A User's Guide to the
VIEW CAMERA

Jim Stone

 HarperCollins*Publishers*

Library of Congress Cataloging-in-Publication Data

Stone, Jim.
    A user's guide to the view camera.

    Includes index.
    1. View cameras. I. Title.
TR258.S67   1987   771'.28'22   86-21040

ISBN 0-673-39617-7

78910-KPK-979695

Cover concept and photography © 1986 by Steve Grohe
Typography by Susan Marsh

Photo credits appear on page 165.

Contents

Preface

What Is This Book About?

A User's Guide to the View Camera will tell you how to make photographs with several kinds of cameras referred to by the generic terms *large-format* and *view camera*. Format means the size and shape of the film used in a camera, and large-format refers to any camera using film larger than 2¼-inch-wide 120 roll film. All of the information about film presented in this book concerns large-format film. View camera is a general name for a group of camera designs in which the lens forms an image directly on a *ground-glass* screen so you can view that image before committing it to film. Almost all view cameras are large-format. And most large-format cameras are view cameras, so the large-format view camera is used as a model for most of the examples in this book. Other kinds of large-format cameras, discussed in Chapter 6, are usually view cameras with some of the features left off to streamline the camera for a specific application.

The characteristic of most view cameras that most differentiates them from other kinds of cameras is that the front and back of the camera are capable of independent movement. And the characteristic of large-format film that makes it most different from small-format film is that it is made and used in sheets, not rolls. A large part of this book is dedicated to an understanding of these unusual features and how they can help you make better pictures. Some view cameras, however, do not incorporate independent movements, and some view cameras that do are not large-format. The province of this book, then, is to introduce you, the photographer, to the use of any camera with large-format film *and* the operation of any camera with a separately adjustable back or front.

Who Is This Book For?

To get the most out of this book, you should already know something about photography. A one-semester black-and-white photography course or its equivalent is a good prerequisite. The chapter on film development, for example, assumes that you have had experience developing roll film; it explains what is different about developing the film used in large-format cameras. This book also assumes that you are familiar, or at least comfortable, with the basics of adjusting and operating hand cameras as it introduces you to the differences (and advantages) of view cameras. If you are learning the basics of photography and the view camera at the same time, you will want to have a good introductory photography book to supplement this one.

In Chapter 2, you will learn about the different parts of the camera—where they are and what they do. Chapter 3 introduces the operation of the camera in its simplest mode; at this point, you will be able to begin to use your camera. With the last half of Chapter 3, you can, at your own pace, add the sophistication of advanced control. Later chapters give you a thorough knowledge of the film systems used in large-format cameras (including the unique Polaroid products), a complete understanding of the lenses you

This 4x5 view camera and 35mm single-lens-reflex camera are both representative examples of their families. Only the use of the larger camera is covered in this book.

will use, a survey of accessories for special purposes, and some advice on maintaining all your large-format camera equipment.

Other than occasional highlights from the history of the camera, all the information presented here is intended to be practical. And although this book may be of interest to the scientist, theoretician, or camera collector, it is meant primarily for you, the photographer.

Acknowledgments

Although this book is credited to a single author, it was a complex collaborative project with assistance, suggestions, and support from a number of generous, capable, and helpful people. Listing them to say thanks is not enough, but it is a start.

In addition to the contributing photographers, and in no particular order, assistance came from Elaine O'Neil, Stanley Rowin, Bob Bretz, Debi Martin, Rob Van Petten, Bruce Kinch, Steve Brettler, Chloe Richfield, Jim Scherer, Bill Crawford, Fred Picker, Henry Horenstein, Beverly and Jack Wilgus, Jon Goell, and Roger Williams. Sheldon Brown, formerly of S. K. Grimes Camera Repair, made me seem an expert on shutters, and Rudolf Kingslake shared his considerable knowledge of lens design and history. The photographs of historic cameras and lenses were made from the monumental private collection assembled by Jack Naylor, with his gracious assistance. Projecting human kindness from inside their corporations were Linda Benedict-Jones, Barbara Hitchcock, Wilma Woollard, and Lou Desiderio of Polaroid; Peter Gowland; Merle and John M. Deardorff; Robert Otis, David Gremp, Richard Carlson, and Richard Lange of Calumet. And thanks go to The Ilex, Linhof, Sinar, Gitzo, Schneider, Wista, and Fuji companies and their distributors. Several teacher/photographers read the manuscript and provided early guidance: David Litschel of Brooks Institute, Bob Thall from Columbia College in Chicago, Rick Steadry from Orange Coast College, and Fred Sway, the Director of the New England School of Photography. Barbara London helped get this book started and past an early derailment. Susan Marsh contributed an elegant design. Liz Hoffman of Graphics Extraordinaire and Tom Briggs of Omnigraphics made the essential drawings; not everything can be photographed. Nancy Benjamin oversaw this book's production and made sure all the words and pictures were the right size and in the right place. Janis Capone put them in those places and, with Nancy, gracefully suffered my meddling in their jobs. Jane Tufts of Little, Brown was the Editor who gave this book form and its author confidence and made sure nothing was left out. Ironically, she was also editing a major text on Psychiatric Nursing as this book hit its frantic final stages. Barbara Anderson helped Jane help me keep the words in order and taught me to know *that* from *which*. Very special thanks are due my parents, Chuck and Sylvia, who started it all, and to Stephanie, who stayed away almost long enough for me to finish.

This book will help you use either of these two unusual cameras — a large-format (4x5) single-lens-reflex on the left and a small-format (35mm) monorail view camera on the right.

A User's Guide to the
VIEW CAMERA

1 Introduction

What Is a Camera?

For an object to be labeled accurately a *camera*, it must have certain basic parts. Common to all cameras is the lighttight body that supports the other parts and prevents unwanted light from striking the film. Integrated into the body is a provision for inserting, holding in place, and removing the film. A lens and shutter admit and control the light, a focusing system adjusts the distance between lens and film, and a viewing system allows you to point the rest of the parts in the right direction. These basic parts are present in the simplest snapshooter (although the focus is often fixed), in the most complex 35mm SLR, and also in a view camera.

A modern modular monorail camera like this Swiss Sinar has a range of interchangeable parts and accessories to help you overcome nearly any photographic challenge.

What Is a View Camera?

A view camera shares its essential anatomy with all cameras, but no other camera type reveals itself as clearly. The view camera's functional skeleton is on display without decorative covering, and none of its basic operating features is obscured by automation. Using the view camera will give you an appreciation and understanding of the bare bones of photographic practice — the fundamentals of making photographs. We will take advantage of this revealed anatomy by using as our model a modular view camera so that we may inspect each part, feature, and application separately.

The modern view camera is a complex and sophisticated system, but it can be broken down into modules, each of which is an individual camera part. Each part is an elemental building block that is interchangeable with other versions of the same part and can be used to assemble and rearrange the camera for a variety of photographic tasks. Since an understanding of these elements is necessary to the proper use of any view camera, Chapter 2 describes the parts of a modular monorail view camera. Details on the rest of the large-format camera family are presented in Chapter 6, after a complete discussion of how to use the monorail camera and following chapters on the lens and film systems common to all large-format cameras. If you are using a camera other than a monorail, you may wish to read the appropriate section of Chapter 6 immediately after Chapter 2.

Why Use a View Camera?

View cameras are heavier, bulkier, and more obtrusive than smaller format cameras, it is time-consuming to set up and use them, and the camera, film, and accessories can be expensive. There must be some considerable advantages to outweigh all of these drawbacks.

Indeed, two important characteristics influence many photographers to use no other camera. First, large-format film renders an image with the highest possible visual qual-

Somerville 17, 1975, *an other-worldly landscape found in the charred ruins of a truck trailer by Carl Chiarenza. Dr. Chiarenza used a Polaroid film-pack adapter (Chapter 8) to have the convenience of instant positive/negative pack film and the advantages of a view camera.*

ity. All the common measures of photographic excellence — sharpness, resolution, tonality, and color saturation — increase with film size. And second, a view camera offers more control over perspective and focus than any other kind of camera. By adjusting the independent front and back of the camera, you can rearrange the position of the vanishing point and the location of the sharpest focus. These advantages would not persuade a photojournalist to use a view camera. To capture the news, a photographer must be unencumbered — free enough and fast enough to follow the action. But for the photographer of the landscape, a subject that waits patiently and motionless for the most flattering light, there is time to set up and use a camera that can deliver the highest possible quality.

The view camera is often considered a professional photographer's tool. Architectural photography, a specialized but well-populated field, demands the control over perspective available only to the user of a view camera. The studio of an advertising, commercial, or portrait photographer is another natural habitat for the view camera. In the studio, everything is arranged for the benefit of the photograph: the scene is assembled, the lighting manipulated, and the moment of exposure selected. After all that, the additional time necessary to set up and use a large camera is slight. The studio photographer leaves nothing in the photograph to chance, and the client who pays for all the care deserves (and usually demands) the superlative quality of an image made on large-format film.

Paradoxically, even the seemingly undesirable characteristics of the view camera are often virtues. Its slow, cumbersome nature forces the photographer to pay close attention to details. Because the entire frame must be studied while focusing, careful composition takes little more time than casual use; the pace encourages care. There are few unpleasant surprises on the processed film. This way of working prompted photographer and art historian Carl Chiarenza to write of the magic of the ground-glass image for the creative photographer:

The view camera photographer is forced into a contemplative mood while he works. Seen in this light the disadvantage of bulky equipment and accessories such as tripods becomes an advantage. It sets the pace for the seclusion under the dark cloth. Facing the ground glass, isolated, all of his facilities are centered on the luminous image. He cannot help being absorbed by the many possible relations he can create within the movable frame. He loses himself in this world of light over which he can exercise a measure of control.

Sometimes the conspicuous use of a view camera enables photographers to make pictures that would not have been available to the user of a hand camera. Bruce Davidson, making the photographs for his landmark book *East 100th Street*, chose a 4x5 camera specifically for its cumbersome nature and obtrusive appearance. Working in a Black and Hispanic ghetto where a stealthy photographer, especially a Caucasian, would be suspect, he chose equipment that would announce his presence and serious intent. "Every day I appeared with my large bellows camera, heavy tripod and box of pictures. Like the TV repairman or organ grinder, I appeared and became part of the street life." The view camera photographer is never taken for an amateur.

You probably already have a reason for learning about the view camera. If not, the unique merits of large-format photography with a view camera will make themselves apparent soon after you make your first exposure.

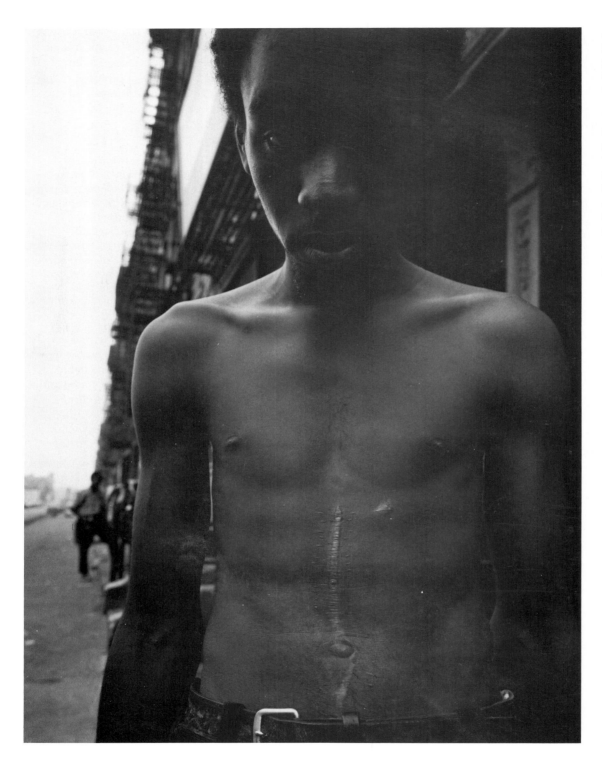

Bruce Davidson made this photograph in 1967 as part of a two-year commitment to documenting what some called the "worst" block in New York City. "The large negative and strobe light made it possible to see with greater depth and sharper detail into the rooms, buildings, vacant lots, streets, and rooftops that defined the space they called their home. The street was a place I would go each day to see the invisible."

Ellen Land-Weber traveled on tour in the People's Republic of China with a light-weight 4x5 field camera and pack film. ". . . There is no way for a Westerner to be a casual, unobtrusive photographer in China. I felt that by using a relatively bulky and time-consuming view camera it would be completely understood what I was doing as a photographer and that I would not offend people. Each time I set up the camera a crowd would gather." She found that inviting people to view through the ground glass was a way to solicit willing subjects for portraits.

2 The Camera

Large-format cameras are categorized by two important features: their format, or nominal film size, and their design. The film size in a camera's designation is usually the largest conventional rectangle the camera can accommodate. These dimensions are given in inches for the U.S. and U.K. and in centimeters for countries that use the metric system. All large-format cameras can be adapted to the use of smaller film, so the nominal film size indicates only the upper limit. A 4x5 camera (called 5x4 in Britain and 10x12 in Germany) can use any size film up to 4-inch by 5-inch film sheets. Other common formats are 5x7 and 8x10.

Two designs dominate today's view camera market: the *flatbed* (in its modern incarnations as *field* (p. 100), *technical* (p. 106), and *press* (p. 105) cameras) and the *monorail* (p. 99). The 4x5 monorail has become the archetypal view camera, and forms the basis for modular camera systems that can be adapted to smaller film as well as modified to become larger-format cameras. Because the individual features of a monorail camera are more obvious than those of any other design, it will be used in this book to exemplify the structure of the generic view camera.

The Monorail View Camera

Named for the supporting shaft at its base, the monorail view camera is the most common of today's large-format cameras. A major characteristic of any view camera is that it provides the physical means to adjust the lens and film positions independently. These adjustments may be made with more freedom and greater ease on a monorail than on a camera of any other design. Inexpensive or student-grade monorail cameras make lens and film position adjustments and provide for interchangeable lenses, but a professional-quality monorail view camera has additional features that make it much more useful.

The versatile, but more expensive, professional monorail cameras are all modular. That is, they comprise a system of interchangeable and interlocking parts and accessories that can be used to assemble a camera tailored to a specific photographic challenge.

The rail clamp attaches to the tripod and provides a solid foundation for the rest of the camera.

Every interlocking module is an elemental camera part that can be moved, extended, or replaced. These elements, common to all view cameras, are described below and illustrated with a modular camera. Familiarize yourself with these parts of the camera and their terminology before trying to set up or use your camera.

Rail

The *rail* provides a rigid base of support for the rest of the camera. Although some rails are round in cross section, some square, and some triangular, the design goal is the same: to provide a light, strong, inflexible shaft along which the adjustable front and back of the camera can slide independently. For most modular cameras the rail can be extended by adding sections. Such extensions would be needed for extreme close-ups and for the use of long-focus lenses. A very short rail for use with short-focus (wide-angle) lenses is also available.

A *rail clamp* holds the rail in place on a tripod and allows you to adjust the position of the rail for balance. The clamp has a threaded hole in its base that matches the corresponding mounting screw on the tripod head (p. 136). The rail slides through the clamp, which may be fixed at any point along the length of the rail. When packing up after a shoot you may choose, if your camera allows it, to remove the camera from its tripod by releasing the clamp from the rail, leaving the clamp attached to the tripod until the next use. This is sometimes easier than removing the clamp from the tripod.

Front and Rear Standards

A *standard* is one of two upright frames attached to the monorail by a sliding geared or spring clamp. Each standard fulfills several functions. The front standard holds the lensboard mounted with lens and shutter at the front of the camera. The rear standard holds the camera's back with its spring back and ground-glass focusing screen, the devices that hold film and determine focus. The bellows is suspended between the two standards. These parts are described in detail later in this chapter. Both standards contain the mechanisms for adjusting independent rotation and movement of the lens or film they hold, and both may be moved longitudinally along the rail. This front-to-back movement is used to vary the distance between the standards and bring an image into focus.

In modular 4x5 cameras the front and rear standards are identical. A monorail camera designed for film larger than 4x5 has a proportionately larger rear standard; its design and function are the same as the front standard's, but the two are not interchange-

The monorail, for which the camera is named, is a rigid tube along which the rest of the camera can slide while maintaining alignment.

The front standard can move along the rail, and contains the mechanisms for adjusting the position of the lens it is designed to support.

Identical to the front standard, the rear standard supports and adjusts the camera back.

able. The spring back of a modular camera is a separate piece, attached with clips to the back of the rear standard. The bellows, also a separate piece, is held to the front of the rear standard with similar or identical clips. The other end of the bellows clips to the back of the front standard, and the front of the front standard holds a separate lensboard. If the attachment mechanisms on both sides of each standard are identical, the standards can be reversed on the rail so the controls are more convenient for a left-handed photographer.

Bellows

The *bellows* is a hollow tube of flexible material held in place between the front and rear standards. With the lensboard and spring back in place, the bellows completes a chamber forming the body of the camera. The *standard* or *square* bellows is made from pleated folds of opaque cloth, leather, or a similar synthetic material, and serves to keep the enclosed volume lighttight without restricting movement of the attached standards for adjustment or focus. The interior surface of the bellows is made nonreflective to assist its accordionlike folds in suppressing contrast-reducing stray light. Unwanted light in-side the camera body can come from the lens projecting an image larger than the film (see *coverage*, p. 74), or from reflections off the film itself. The standard bellows collapses compactly for storage and can be extended enough for all but the most extreme long-focus lens or close-up work.

Spring Back

The back of a view camera is formed by the *spring back*, a pair of nesting frames on the rear standard. It holds the ground glass in place for focusing and viewing, and it accepts a film holder for exposure. The ground glass is held in the inner frame, which in turn is held to the outer frame by springs. As the film holder slides into place between the two frames, it forces the ground-glass frame away from the rest of the camera back. The holder is pressed securely into place against the inner frame by the springs, forming a lightproof seal. The spring back's dual role — holding both ground glass and film — is important because it enables the position of the film during exposure to correspond exactly to the position of the ground glass during viewing. The image can then be recorded exactly as viewed.

The bellows attaches between the standards and allows them freedom of movement while forming an opaque and lighttight shell.

The camera back clips into the rear standard and contains the spring back to hold the film and the ground glass to allow focusing.

The lensboard, with its attached lens and shutter, is held in place in the front standard.

Like many modular view cameras, this Horseman 450 allows its standards to be reversed on the rail for the convenience of a left-handed photographer.

A modular, system view camera like this Toyo allows the use of several different-sized film backs with the same rail and front standard. To change formats, the bellows, rear standard, and back must be replaced.

A bail lever is sometimes incorporated into the spring back to facilitate the insertion of film holders.

Removing the spring back from this universal (or Graflok) back allows other accessory backs to be clipped into place.

Some view cameras have a *bail lever* around the ground-glass frame to force the springs apart and open a path for the film holder. This prevents the unnecessary wear on your film holders that occurs if they are forced into place by using them to pry the ground-glass frame away from the camera back.

On many 4x5 cameras, the spring back is held with clips in yet another frame and can be removed to allow the use of various accessory backs and film holders. Graflex introduced this modular design in 1949 as the *Graflok* back on Speed Graphic cameras. Although camera backs bearing the Graflok brand name are no longer manufactured, current *universal* or *international* backs are interchangeable with them and Graflok-style accessories will fit them all.

A *revolving* back allows you to rotate the spring back and ground glass to any desired position in its outer frame. This feature enables you to avoid having to rotate a large camera to frame a photograph exactly as you want. A *reversing* back fits into the rear standard either horizontally or vertically, but adjustments of the film's orientation for angles in between must be made by rotating the en-

With a revolving back you can position the image between horizontal and vertical without tipping the camera into a precarious position.

tire camera, using the tripod head. Revolving backs are rare on cameras larger than 4x5; these most often use the lighter and more compact reversing back to save considerable bulk.

Ground Glass

The frame of the spring back holds in place a sheet of *ground glass* on which you view, compose, and focus the image projected by the lens. Ground glass is sheet glass made translucent by grinding, etching, or sanding one surface. The ground side of the glass faces the lens to receive the image, inverted by the lens, and the glass sheet should be the exact size and shape of the film. The position the front surface of the ground glass holds during viewing and focusing should be the exact position held by the film's emulsion when the ground glass is moved away by a film holder in place for exposure. See Chapter 8 for more information on the ground glass.

Lensboard

A *lensboard* is the rigid, opaque plate that holds the lens to the front standard. Most lensboards are flat, square panels of metal or wood drilled with a single mounting hole for the lens. The back or interior side of the lensboard should be nonreflective black so that it can absorb light reflected from the film during exposure.

Many wooden cameras use wooden lensboards, and you can fabricate and drill a substitute yourself with hand tools to save money. The more modern, modular monorail cameras have metal lensboards with formed edges that are difficult to duplicate in a home shop. These metal lensboards are rarely interchangeable from one brand of camera to another. And although you will need one for each lens you wish to use on your view camera, lensboards are sold separately from the lenses.

Lens and Shutter

A *lens* gathers the light in front of it and converges that light to a focus behind it to form an image. The lens for a view camera is recognizable as a lens to anyone familiar with other cameras. It is larger than most other lenses, however, and is usually mounted in a *shutter*. As in other cameras, the shutter opens and closes to admit light to the film for a metered amount of time. Before you can use your camera, the shutter and lens must be mounted to the lensboard in a round mounting hole and the lensboard must be affixed to the front standard. Lens mounting is a job usually left to a specialist in a camera repair or machine shop. If you want more information about lenses at this point, read Chapters 5 and 7.

3 Using Your Camera

Now that you are familiar with the structure of your camera, you can begin to put it to use. Establishing a familiar pattern of use with your camera will enable you to set it up and adjust it while concentrating on the image you wish to make. Initially, setting up the camera will demand your undivided attention, so before you take it out into traffic, practice setting up and adjusting your camera in a place where you can work comfortably and without distraction.

This chapter is designed to get you working with your camera as soon as possible. First we will move through the making of a simple exposure and the sequence of actions you must follow for every photograph. Using the camera this way will be very much like using a bigger version of a camera you already know, and you will soon become comfortable with the essentials of view camera use. The latter part of the chapter will introduce you to the way the camera movements influence and control perspective and focus. Mastering the camera movements is difficult and should be left until you are comfortable with the basics of using the camera.

Many of the camera parts and accessories mentioned here are explained in detail later, so you can read through this sequence of steps rapidly, without digression. If you want more complete information, refer to the page numbers indicated.

Mounting the Camera

Before mounting the camera on your *tripod* (p. 134), extend the tripod's legs so that its platform is at chest height. This positioning places the tripod's feet far apart to give you a steady platform for attaching the camera. It also places the ground-glass viewing screen at a comfortable height just below eye level. Save lower camera positions for a time when you are proficient and can set up and work quickly — prolonged viewing in low positions can strain your lower back. After a little ex-

perience, you will know in advance how much to extend the tripod's legs for the vantage point you desire. Remember that the height of the platform is much easier to adjust before you have the weight of the camera on it.

Locate the threaded mounting bolt projecting through the platform of your *tripod head* (p. 136) and the corresponding threaded hole in your camera's rail clamp or baseplate. With one hand hold the camera as close to its top as possible while aligning and threading the mounting screw into the hole in the baseplate with your other hand. Make sure the rail, or lens axis, is aligned with the axis of the tripod head before you tighten the mounting screw securely. Many cameras have a carrying handle at the top of the rear standard, which makes the mounting operation much easier. Never hold a view camera in one hand by its monorail — this is an invitation for the camera to invert and crash into the tripod or worse, onto the ground.

Before you release your grip on the camera and rely upon the tripod for safe support, be sure all the adjustment levers on the tripod head are secure. If just one lever works loose, the camera may tip and capsize the entire tripod. Check also to make sure the lens and lensboard are securely attached before you move or tilt the camera. The most convenient way to move the camera more than a few steps is to lean it over your shoulder, but this rifle-carry position places considerable strain on the mount. If the camera comes loose, a fall from shoulder height could irreparably damage both camera and lens.

Positioning the Camera

Swivel the tripod head to align the axis of the monorail and lens with one leg of the tripod. This position, with one tripod leg pointed forward, will give you room to move around behind the camera between the other two legs without continually kicking or trip-

The lens projects an image upside down onto the ground-glass viewing screen. To see it well, your eye should be about the same distance from it as a comfortable reading distance from a book page the same size.

Zero Position

Zero position for a view camera means that all of its adjustments are set as though it were a rigid-bodied camera: front and rear standards are parallel to one another and at right angles to the monorail, and the rear of the lens is pointed straight at the center of the ground glass. This neutral setting is sometimes called the *normal* position.

Once your camera is mounted on its tripod, set all the movements to zero position and extend the bellows by setting the standards approximately one focal length apart, that is, 150mm (6 inches) apart with a 150mm lens. This setting, called the *infinity focus*, is a good place to start for general work. The bellows will need to be extended further for close-ups. Make sure the camera's movements, standards, clamps, and revolving back are securely locked.

Framing and Focusing

To view through your camera, open the shutter using the *press-focus lever* (p. 88) and set the aperture to its widest setting. Then, facing your subject, stand behind the ground glass. Cover your head and the rear standard with the *darkcloth* (p. 139) and look at the image that appears upside-down on the ground glass. All lenses invert the image they form but other cameras are designed to reinvert the image (*reflex* cameras) or else provide an alternate upright image (such as a *viewfinder* image) for you to look at. Remember, in a view camera you are looking *at* the ground glass, not through it, so your eyes will need to be reading-distance away from it. In time, you will find it as easy to work with an image upside-down as with one right-side-up.

After you open the shutter, disengage the focus lock on the rear standard and focus on the scene by moving the rear standard along the rail. Your camera will probably have a focus knob to move the standard by very small amounts. Focus by rocking the knob back and forth past the point you think is the best focus a few times, rocking it less and less each time until you settle on the position for best focus. If you have a fast lens, that is, one with a large maximum aperture, it will admit enough light for you to focus unassisted in bright light, but at smaller apertures and for very precise focusing, hold a magnifying *loupe*

ping over one tripod leg. It will also provide a more stable platform should you tilt the camera downward.

It is not practical to take frequent casual glances through a view camera the way you might with a 35mm, to decide on the correct camera position for the image you desire. Instead you will need to train your eye to see what the camera sees. With time you will be able to place the tripod in its final position the first time you set it down. For now, place the tripod approximately and point the camera in the general direction for the photograph you plan to make.

(p. 157) against the ground glass to enlarge a part of the image. Make certain the front of the monorail is not visible in the image at the top of the ground glass. If it is, move the front standard forward on the rail, then refocus. If after viewing the image you decide to change it by moving the camera (or, later, if you change the camera movements), you will also need to refocus.

Although under most circumstances you can adjust the focus equally well with either the front or rear standard, get in the habit of focusing with the rear standard. It is especially difficult to focus close up with the front standard because it changes the magnification and makes the image larger or smaller as you focus. This change results from altering the distance from lens to subject — the *object distance*. Using the rear standard to focus allows you to find the appropriate focus for an object in a fixed relation to the lens. With a very short object distance it is often easier to move the entire camera or even the subject to bring the image into precise focus.

Lock the focus knob in place after final focusing. Select your working aperture by stopping down until adequate depth of field is visible in the ground glass. These adjustments are judged strictly by eye, so you will need to manipulate the controls from the rear of the camera, while under the darkcloth. When the camera is adjusted and focused, and the lens is stopped down to the working aperture, close the shutter. After taking your exposure reading, set and wind the shutter. You may wish at this point to check exposure, lighting, framing, and focus with a sheet of Polaroid film (p. 145).

Making the Exposure

Once you are certain the camera and tripod have been properly adjusted and all of the parts have been locked in place, open the spring back. If your camera has one, use the bail lever. If not, pry back the ground-glass frame a bit with your fingers and insert a loaded *film holder* (p. 60.) against the spring pressure. Hold the camera steady to avoid moving it out of position. With some cameras it may be easier to remove the entire back, insert the holder, then replace the back. If you are using the bail lever, release it gently to prevent the back from snapping shut and cracking the ground glass. The film holder

To begin using your camera, set it securely on its tripod, and make sure all the adjustments are locked in zero position and the shutter is opened for viewing.

With the darkcloth covering your head and the camera's back, focus the image on the ground glass by moving the rear standard along the rail.

After closing the shutter, insert a film holder and withdraw its darkslide. Make sure the camera is motionless before gently pressing the cable release to make the exposure.

must make a good lighttight seal to avoid unwanted streaks on the film or fogging (*fog* is an even, overall exposure to unfocused light that lowers contrast and degrades the image quality). If you are unfamiliar with your camera, you may have trouble at first finding this proper, seated position. Practice inserting and removing the film holder a few times to make sure you know where the holder is supposed to seat.

Double-check the shutter to see that it is closed and then gently withdraw the *darkslide* (p. 61) from the side of the film holder facing the lens. In dry climates, a too-rapid movement of the darkslide may generate enough static electricity to mark the film. If the sun is shining on the camera back, or if there will be a long delay between removing the darkslide and making the exposure, drape the darkcloth over the camera back to protect against possible light leaks.

Look carefully at the camera for vibration. If you have just taken your hands away from it, give it time to stop moving. If there is a breeze against the bellows, try to wait for a lull. Hold the end of the *cable release* (p. 138) in your hand, leaving enough slack in the cable to prevent motion being transmitted from you to the camera. Make the exposure by pressing the cable release to trigger the shutter. After the exposure is made, insert the darkslide back into the holder with the black rim of its handle facing the outside (a safeguard signifying exposed film) and remove the film holder from the camera.

Your view camera's unique appearance is in part the result of its separately adjustable front and rear standards. *Camera movements*, the adjustments of these standards, make the view camera unique in function as well as appearance. The importance of adjustable standards is that we can use them to independently alter and control the positions of the lens plane and film plane.

The *film plane* is the position of the film during exposure, or of the front surface of the ground glass without the film holder in place. With a movable rear standard, the film plane can be angled away from its normal position perpendicular to the rail and to the *optical axis*, the path of a ray of light passing unrefracted through the center of the lens.

The *lens plane* is always perpendicular to the optical axis, and corresponds roughly to the position of the lensboard (it may in fact be slightly in front of or behind the board depending on the kind of lens and the thickness of the board and lens mount). With the front standard's movements, the lens plane may be moved away from its normal position perpendicular to the rail. The optical axis moves with the lens.

Moving the lens and film planes away from their normal positions parallel to each other changes the rendering on film of both perspective and focus. Once you are in control of the effects of these movements, you can create images that would otherwise be impossible. Because the idea of camera

Adding the camera movements to your photographic repertoire will give you pictorial control otherwise impossible, as shown in this photograph by Switzerland's Fred Waldvogel made for Sinar on their 5x7 Model P camera.

The film plane extends in all directions, continuing outward from the edges of the film, or the front surface of the ground glass.

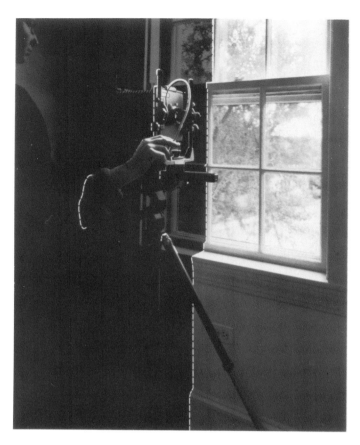

The lens plane extends the surface of the lensboard. It is always perpendicular to the optical axis.

The optical axis is an imaginary line through the center of the lens, perpendicular to the lens plane.

movements may be new to you, it may seem intimidating at first. Finish reading this chapter entirely before trying to apply the concepts it introduces. You will need to understand how the camera movements change an image before you can successfully apply that knowledge. Then put your camera through its paces while rereading this chapter. In a short time you will be able to concentrate on the ground-glass image while setting the movements, using no more conscious thought than you need to adjust the focus.

Always begin with your camera set up in zero (or normal) position with the monorail or camera base horizontal and the lensboard and camera back vertical. The lens plane (lensboard) and film plane (camera back) should be parallel, so that the optical axis will run parallel to the monorail through the center of the lens and the center of the ground glass. Get into the habit of returning the camera to the zero position after each photograph.

Swings and Tilts

Adjusting the front and rear standards to control the image requires some combination of three motions: shift, swing, and tilt. These camera movements are adjustments of the plane and position of the lens and film and are sometimes referred to as swings and tilts.

A *tilt* is a movement of the lens plane or film plane around a horizontal axis perpendicular to the optical axis. Nodding your head as if to answer yes would be a tilt of your face.

A *swing* is a movement of the lens or film plane around a vertical axis perpendicular to the optical axis. Shaking your head to say no is a face swing. Swings and tilts are both inclining movements and produce an angular change in the position of the lens or film plane.

A movement of the lens or ground glass that leaves it in the same plane is called a *shift*. For example, in a lens shift you would slide the lens to the side or up or down and produce a lateral or vertical displacement of the optical axis. Opening a sliding door is a shift movement. A vertical shift is often called a *rise* or *fall*.

What the Movements Do

The camera movements increase your ability to control two important aspects of a photograph: the rendering of perspective and the position of the plane of focus through the image. *Perspective* means the relative sizes of objects in the image, and the *plane of focus* is that plane in front of the lens in which all points are in focus, independent of depth of field. Although the effects of front and back movements can overlap (shifting the front up gives almost exactly the same results as shifting the back down), and although a single movement of one standard can affect both plane of focus and perspective, the swings and tilts are best understood if you mentally separate the functions of the front and back. As a rule of thumb, *use the position of the lens plane to control plane of focus and the position of the back to control perspective*.

The camera in zero (or normal) position.

The illustrations on the next few pages show the camera movements — swing, tilt, and shift — shown in extreme positions for clarity. In normal use, you will rarely need to adjust your camera so far from zero position.

Front tilt, sometimes called lens tilt.

Back tilt.

Front or lens swing.

Back swing.

Vertical lens shift, nearly always called front rise.

Vertical lens shift: front fall.

Front or lens shift.

Back rise.

The actual positions of the lens and film will affect your photograph, not how you got them into those positions. The effect on your photograph of a front and back tilt on an inclined rail . . .

. . . is exactly the same as the effect from a front rise on a horizontal rail.

Controlling Perspective: Back Movements

In your past experience as a photographer, you have probably found that one of the most important controls at your disposal is camera placement. This may seem obvious; if you put the camera in the forest, you will make a different photograph than you would in the city. And a photograph made from above your head will be different from one made at knee level. These considerations of *vantage point* are extremely important to the making of photographs with any camera.

Vantage point is the position of the lens in space and determines *perspective*, that is, the relative sizes of near and far objects in your image. Perspective is also the relative sizes of near and far parts of the same object so, as a direct consequence, perspective con-

In this 1969 photograph of New York City buildings, Harry Callahan made intentional use of the keystone effect, *the convergence of vertical lines that is a natural consequence of tilting the camera up.*

trols the appearance of the shape of objects. The perspective in your photograph will ordinarily be the same as what you would see with one eye if it were viewing the scene from the same position as the lens. If you can alter the position of the back of a camera, and therefore the position of the film relative to the optical axis, you can alter this apparent perspective in your photographs. Once you have placed your lens for the desired vantage point, your view camera allows you to control the appearance of the image further by altering the position of the back.

Back Tilt

As an example of the kind of perspective control a view camera can give you, use a 35mm camera (or any camera having back and lens in fixed positions) at ground level to photograph all of a tall building. The building, having vertical, parallel sides, will appear in the photograph to be narrower at the top. This effect, called the *keystone effect*, is the result of tilting the camera up to include the top of the building. The top of the building appears smaller than the bottom because it is farther from the lens and the parallel sides of the building appear to converge toward the top.

To avoid the keystone effect with your view camera, you can tilt, or incline, the back independently of the rest of the camera. When you do, one end or edge of the film ends up closer to the lens than the other. The cone of light projected rearward by the lens (p. 31) gets larger as it moves away from the lens. When you incline the film plane, the image on the part of the film farther from the

An earlier photograph by Callahan, from Dearborn Street in Chicago, 1948, exhibits vertical lines of the building carefully made to appear exactly vertical in the photograph. Callahan's mastery of the camera allows him to select and control convergence to his own aesthetic advantage.

lens becomes larger than that part closer to the lens. This tilt will diminish the appearance of convergence toward that side of the image.

Because the lens inverts the image, the top of the building in the example above appears at the bottom of the ground glass. Tilting the back, now leaning with its top away from the building, toward a vertical position moves the image of the top of the building (seen at the bottom of the ground glass) away from the lens, making it larger or wider, and the image of its bottom (at the top of the ground glass) toward the lens, making it smaller or narrower. If the back is adjusted this way until the top and bottom of the building appear to be the same width in the image, its sides will appear both vertical and parallel.

This tilting procedure alters the normal perspective of the image. Your eye, like a fixed-back camera, actually forms an image of the building with its top narrower. Your brain usually ignores that data, however, because you *know* the sides of the building are parallel. Some photographers refer to this kind of perspective alteration in a photograph as "correcting," because it makes the image appear as we *perceive* the building, not as we *see* it.

Photographs of buildings are the most obvious examples of the need for this kind of perspective control. When architects and builders carefully design and construct buildings having parallel sides they like to see their efforts clearly demonstrated in photographs of their buildings. They exhibit a particularly strong preference when they are paying for the photographs.

The Vanishing Point and Convergence. When you make photographs, remember first that the relative sizes of near and far objects (and of near and far parts of the same object) are determined by where you place your lens. The *vanishing point* is the point at which parallel lines or surfaces receding from the camera position appear to converge. Because tilting the back increases or diminishes convergence, it also moves the vanishing point closer to or farther away from the center of the image. Once you have selected a specific vantage point, you may further modify the perspective by altering the location of the apparent vanishing point with the position of the camera's back.

Tilting the back controls vertical convergence. When the camera back is vertical, all vertical lines in the scene appear as parallel vertical lines in the photograph. If the back is tilted away from vertical, as in the previous example with the tall building, vertical lines in the scene will converge in the photograph. If convergence is desired, as in the photograph of the loudspeakers on the opposite page, it can be exaggerated; the farther from vertical the back is tilted, the greater the convergence.

Note that increased convergence means that the vanishing point moves closer to the center of the image. The results of tilting the back are easiest to understand by looking at vertical lines, such as building sides in an architectural photograph. But even in an image containing no straight lines, such as a landscape, moving the vanishing point profoundly affects the appearance of the photograph.

Opposite: Vertical convergence was exaggerated with back tilt for dramatic emphasis in this advertising photograph made for the loudspeaker manufacturer by Geoff Stein.

Pointing the camera straight at a tall building from eye level will result in a photograph that includes a great deal of foreground but lacks the top of the building.

Pointing the camera up to center the building in the frame results in a photograph that shows the sides of the building as converging lines. The bottom of the building is closer to the camera than the top, and is represented in normal perspective by appearing larger.

Tilting the back of the camera moves the bottom of the camera, with the image of the top of the building, farther from the lens than the top of the camera with the image of the bottom of the building. The image formed by the lens grows larger as it moves back away from the lens in the projected cone of light, so the image of the building's top is made larger to appear the same width as the image of the bottom of the building.

These three photographs were made from the same camera position and show the effects of back tilt on vertical convergence and the location of the vanishing point.

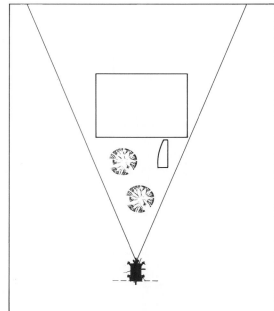

The front of this building shows its horizontal lines parallel (without horizontal convergence) because it was made from a position exactly in front of the building's center. Unfortunately, there is also a tree in a position exactly in front of the building, making the value of this vantage point questionable.

Back Swing

While back tilt controls vertical convergence, back swing affects convergence (the position of the vanishing point) for horizontal lines. When a horizontal line on the back of the camera is parallel to horizontal lines in your subject, as in a head-on photograph of a house, the horizontal lines in the image will all be parallel and horizontal. Pointing the camera at the same house from a position on either side of head-on, with the camera back at an oblique angle to the front of the house, the horizontal lines will converge away from the camera. Swinging the back from this position to be more parallel with the front of the house will reduce this convergence; swinging it farther away from parallel will exaggerate it.

In the two series of photos on the following pages, placing the camera in position for a head-on photograph eliminates convergence as easily as using the back swing. The swing movement is most useful when your access to a desired vantage point is limited, for example by a tree or car in front of the house. This is why the back tilt is more often used than the swing; a vantage point head-on to a horizontal surface is easier to achieve (say, by walking around a building) than one head-on to a vertical surface (which might require a very tall ladder). Your own mobility is often much greater horizontally than vertically.

The advantages of swing and tilt control are most evident when you are photographing man-made objects because their regular shapes make convergence more noticeable. This is why the view camera is indispensable when photographing architecture or for advertising. Remember that nature's forms are no less affected by moving the vanishing point, however, and creative control is at your fingertips when using a view camera for landscapes.

From a vantage point slightly to the side, the building's elevation is clearly visible, the tree is on the left edge of the frame, but the horizontal lines converge to the left.

By using a back swing, making the back parallel to the building's facade, the horizontal lines are made parallel in the photograph made from this vantage point.

These three photographs made from exactly the same camera position show that back swing can be used to introduce and control horizontal convergence, without altering the vantage point.

Timothy O'Sullivan made this photograph of Colorado's Vermillion Creek Canyon in 1872 for the United States Geological Survey.

For the Rephotographic Survey Project, Mark Klett made this photograph in 1979 from O'Sullivan's original vantage point showing this particular section of our western landscape to be virtually unchanged in over a century.

Klett's precise methodology reveals O'Sullivan's use of camera movements for perspective alteration. This Polaroid field check of camera position made without camera movements has the borders of O'Sullivan's photograph drawn in. Their trapezoidal shape indicates that an angular displacement of the camera back is necessary to recreate the perspective shown in the 1872 photograph.

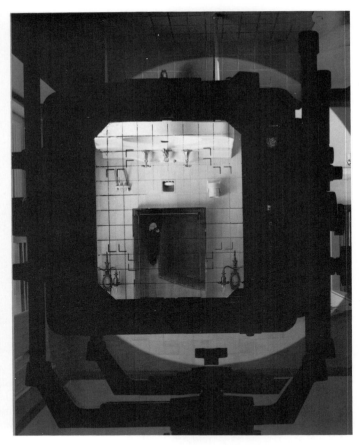

Without camera movements, a head-on photograph of this environ-
ment reveals the camera's reflection in the mirror.

Moving the camera to the side removes the reflection in the mirror,
and the image circle from the lens is large enough to allow a back
shift to adjust the framing of the image.

Back Shift

Back shift movements — rising, falling, and
lateral shifts — do not alter the perspective of
the image, but they do alter the image in
other ways. Think of the image projected by
your view camera lens onto the film as the
one projected by a slide projector onto a
screen. If the slide projector is too far from
the screen, the image you see on the screen
is only part of the image on the slide — the
extra spills over the edges of the screen. By
moving the screen from side to side and up
and down, you can make different pictures
appear on the screen, each a different section
of the whole slide.

In a similar manner, most view camera
lenses project an image somewhat larger than
the film (see *coverage*, p. 74), and you can
shift the back of your camera side to side and
up and down to select the desired part of that
larger image. In this way you can make adjustments to the framing of an image without
moving the entire camera and with no
change in perspective or vantage point.

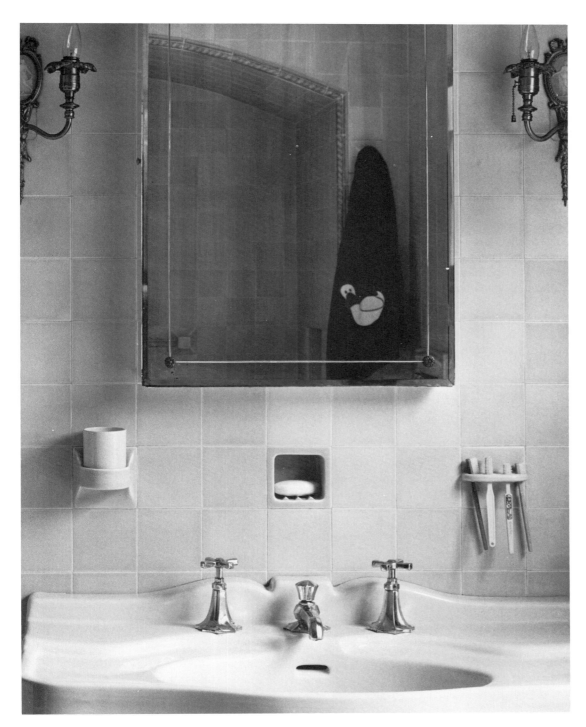

The resulting image avoids the camera's reflection in the mirror yet still allows the pattern of tiles to be reproduced without convergence.

Controlling Plane of Focus: Lens Movements

With a rigid-bodied camera such as a 35mm, the lens plane and film plane are parallel and fixed in relation to each other. The only relative movement allowed is changing the distance between the two to focus. When this distance is adjusted so that a point 2 meters from the lens is in focus, an entire plane through that point, parallel to the lens and film planes, is in focus as well. Adjusting the focus to 3 meters moves this *plane of focus* 1 meter farther away. This plane of focus is always a two-dimensional surface slicing through a three-dimensional world.

When your view camera's lens plane and film plane are parallel, the plane of focus behaves in exactly the same way as that of any rigid-bodied camera. You have the option, however, to adjust the lens and film planes away from their normal parallel position. A swing or tilt of either lens or back will move the plane of focus to a new position parallel to neither lens nor film plane. Understanding and applying this control will make it possible for you to make great photographs in otherwise impossible situations. If, for example, you were photographing across a tilled field, with your camera aimed at the horizon, tilting the lens plane by moving the top of the lensboard forward would move the plane of focus to cut horizontally across the surface of the entire field. In this way you would have the entire field in focus, foreground to background, without having to use a very small aperture to get great depth of field. The larger working aperture would allow the use of a faster shutter speed, perhaps to stop the action of workers moving in the field. In addition, the wider apertures (but not the widest) of any lens will usually produce an image with greater sharpness than the smaller apertures on the same lens.

In the following section, you will learn how the angle between the lens plane and film plane determines the position of the plane of focus. When you change that angle by moving either lens or film plane, you will change the plane of focus. In the previous section we found that perspective depends on vantage point and can be altered by the position of the film plane. Perspective is not altered by angular movements (swing or tilt) of the lens plane. Because of this, your chosen perspective will be unaffected by your adjusting the plane of focus if you make that ad-

Set up in zero position and focused on the single large jet in the back, the plane of focus is vertical; the limited depth of field throws the foreground out of focus. The appearance and position of the plane of focus are the same as they would be using any hand camera.

With the lens tilted so that the lens plane and film plane meet in a line with the horizontal plane of the tabletop, the plane of focus is now horizontal, leaving the vertical jet out of focus. The position of the back of the camera and therefore the rendering of perspective remains unchanged.

justment with the lens plane and not with the back. To save steps, select your vantage point first, then adjust convergence with the back, and finally alter the lens plane if you wish to move the position of the plane of focus.

The Scheimpflug Principle

When the lens and film planes are *not* parallel to each other (a situation usually possible only with a view camera), an unusual set of optical conditions exists in which the plane of focus cuts at an angle through the image. The rule governing this peculiar situation was named after a Prussian army officer of the nineteenth century who was presumably the first to quantify the results. The *Scheimpflug* (shīm'-floog) *Principle* states that when the lens plane and film plane are not parallel, neither will be parallel to the plane of focus. Fortunately, the Scheimpflug Principle also tells us where the plane of focus will be: it will meet the lens plane and film plane in a line.

Front Tilt

To visualize the effects of the Scheimpflug Principle, imagine your camera set up in zero position. If you stand close to the camera back, the film plane passes through your toes (remember the film *plane* doesn't stop at the edges of the film). If you tilt the lensboard forward so that its extended surface (the lens plane) also passes through your toes, and you adjust the focus properly, then the plane of focus will be the floor. In other words, with the back vertical and the lens tilted forward, the surface of the floor will be entirely in focus—the plane of focus will be horizontal. The planes of the lens, film, and floor meet in a horizontal line, perpendicular to the rail, at your toes.

Front Swing

If you set your camera at an oblique angle to a long wall, you can swing the front standard so that the lens plane meets the vertical line where the film plane cuts the wall. The surface of the wall will then be the plane of focus. In this way, the plane of focus may be made to lie along any vertical, flat surface.

Once you get used to the notion that the plane of focus needn't be parallel to the film, and can visualize the positions of the film plane and lens plane beyond the edges of the ground glass and lensboard, it will be easy for you to use the Scheimpflug Principle to your advantage.

Front Shift

Shifting the front in one direction has almost exactly the same effect as shifting the back in the opposite direction. A lens shift, however, introduces a change in vantage point. For a distant scene, moving the vantage point only a few centimeters will not produce a noticeable change in the image, so you can often use a front rise interchangeably with a back fall. In situations where small adjustments of vantage point are needed, such as close-up work, use the lens shift for exact placement of the vantage point, then use the back shift to adjust the exact framing of the desired image.

Depth of Field

Theoretically, a lens can only focus sharply on a flat, two-dimensional surface, the plane of focus. In practice, however, your eye is unable to distinguish between the sharpness in the image formed of a point in the plane of focus and that of one slightly closer or farther which is only slightly unfocused. The distance between the near and far limits of

This diagram shows the limits of the depth of field at several aperture settings, around a plane of focus repositioned using the Scheimpflug Principle. Though the plane of focus has been repositioned by a lens shift, as it is here, and this diagram looks quite different from what you might be used to, the behavior of the depth of field is essentially unchanged by the Scheimpflug Principle.

In this 1981 photograph, Charles Roitz tilted the lens of his 8x10 view camera to make the plane of focus run along the surface of the ground. With intentionally limited depth of field, the focused area slips under the roadside fence, leaving it suspended in a slight blur.

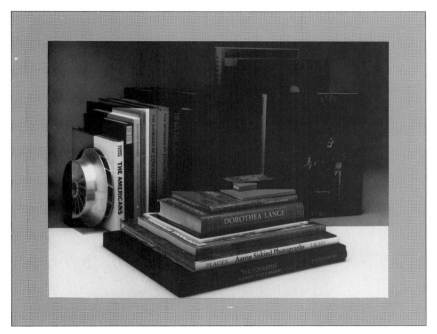

With the camera in zero position, the plane of focus cuts through these books vertically. With a normal lens and at this vantage point, it would be impossible to achieve enough depth of field to include both foreground and background in focus.

By tilting the lens according to the Scheimpflug Principle, the plane of focus was tilted to cut through this image from lower foreground to upper background so that all the objects could be brought into focus with the minimum depth of field. In this case, closing the aperture by only two stops was sufficient. Using the Scheimpflug Principle allows you to find and use the most advantageous position for the plane of focus in any photograph.

what we see in the image to be in focus is the *depth of field* and it is always measured perpendicular to the plane of focus. Depth of field affects the appearance of your photographs profoundly by determining what appears to be in focus; it therefore deserves careful attention during the making of any photograph.

With your view camera in zero position, the behavior of the depth of field conforms to the same rules it obeys in any rigid-bodied camera. The lens and film planes are parallel, and the near and far limits of the depth of field are planes parallel to the lens plane, the film plane, and the plane of focus. For a given object distance (from the lens to the plane of focus), the distance included in the depth of field will increase with smaller apertures. For a given aperture, depth of field will increase for greater object distances. For very short object distances, the plane of focus is near the center of the depth of field. There is an old adage about the plane of focus having one-third of the depth of field in front of it (toward the camera) and two-thirds behind it; this is generally accurate at middle distances (say, across the room or across the street). At greater distances, the depth of field increases to a much greater extent behind the plane of focus than in front of it.

The behavior of the depth of field is altered by the Scheimpflug Principle, though not beyond recognition. Depth of field still is increased by smaller apertures and greater object distances, and still surrounds the plane of focus. Since all parts of the plane of focus are not at the same distance from the lens, however, the depth of field is not the same in all parts of the image. Depth of field increases as the plane of focus recedes from the camera. At smaller apertures, it increases more rapidly with distance.

Depth of field is affected by aperture, object distance, and lens plane adjustments, but it depends especially upon what is considered acceptable sharpness for your use. Judgment of acceptable sharpness is subjective, and hinges on such factors as viewing distance and degree of enlargement for the final print. To supplement experience for increasing your ability to make judgments about depth of field, there are standard tables and scales based on average values of the factors affecting depth of field. This information may be found explained in detail in a standard text on photographic optics.

The lens swing was used to line up the plane of focus with one face of this pile of hay bales, and then with the other face from the same camera position. A wide aperture limited the depth of field so that the positions of the plane of focus are easily visible.

More About Perspective

As in a painting or any other two-dimensional pictorial representation, the illusion of depth in a photograph depends upon four factors: 1. *Atmospheric effect* is the softening of detail with distance, as though the scene were viewed in a haze. In a photograph it is controlled by your selection of film and filters, time of day, and focus. 2. *Lighting* can be controlled in the studio or selected outdoors to give the illusion of compressed or expanded distance. Soft, nondirectional light, for example, compresses distance. 3. *Interposition of objects*, the way a foreground object hides what is behind it, is primary information for the eye in judging relative distances. An object with its contour interrupted by that of another object appears to be behind the object interrupting it. 4. *Linear perspective*, the relative sizes of objects in the image, causes objects in the foreground to appear larger than objects of similar size in the distance.

Linear perspective is wholly the result of vantage point (lens position). The closer you position your lens to an object, the larger it will appear in relation to objects behind it. The effects of linear perspective are independent of lens focal length (p. 79), even though you might assume that a wide-angle lens will render a different perspective from that of a long-focus lens. This misconception results from the fact that a wide-angle lens must be much closer to an object to make the image of that object the same size on a negative. The closer position changes the perspective by making other, distant objects relatively smaller, hence the assumption that shorter lenses exaggerate perspective. From the same camera position, however, all lenses will represent objects in the same relative sizes.

This photograph of the John F. Kennedy Memorial Library was made with a wide-angle lens, in this case a 90mm lens on a 4x5 camera.

Made with a 180mm lens from exactly the same camera position, therefore an identical vantage point, this photograph shows every part of the image to be exactly twice as large as the one made with a lens having half the focal length.

Making a photograph with the 90mm lens to include the same boundaries as one with the 180mm lens requires a much closer camera position (vantage point); therefore the perspective appears completely different. This rendering of perspective is not the result of using a wide-angle lens, but is because of the close position.

Enlarging the center section of the first wide-angle photograph (upper left) gives exactly the same perspective as that rendered by the longer lens from the same position. Perspective depends entirely upon vantage point and not at all upon focal length.

Setting Up a Photograph:
A Complete Sequence

After you have read the section on lenses (Chapter 5), and if you are fortunate enough to have a selection of lenses from which to choose, a simple sequence of steps can lead you to exactly the photograph you want. You will eventually integrate these steps into your procedure for setting up the camera, and your mind will be free to concentrate on the desired image.

1. Select a vantage point for the desired perspective. Where you put the lens and when you make the exposure are the most important decisions you must make for each photograph. Remember that the selection of a lens is not a factor in the control of perspective; if you close one eye you will see objects in the same relative size — with the same linear perspective — as with any lens you choose. The vantage point is determined entirely by the position of the lens; use the placement of the camera as a rough control and the lens shift for fine-tuning.

2. Select the focal length of the lens for the *angle of view* (p. 80), the section of the scene in front of the lens you wish to include. If you don't have the exact lens you need, you can use a shorter focal-length lens (one having a wider angle of view) and plan to crop out the unwanted part of the image later. If you substitute a longer lens (one with a smaller angle of view) it will leave out part of the desired image, or force you to move the camera farther back. If you move the camera you will change the size relationships you determined in selecting your vantage point.

3. Once you have selected a lens and established a perspective based upon a specific vantage point, adjust the back to contour the perspective to your needs. By combining tilt and swing movements you can adjust convergence (move the vanishing point) not only horizontally and vertically but to any angle in between. More often than not you will want the back vertical. This is such a common working position that many cameras provide a small bubble level — often two — on the rear standard to aid in determining a precisely vertical position. If your camera is not so

To determine exactly how much to tilt the lens for your selected plane of focus, you should approach the correct setting gradually, in steps. Pick a point in the foreground and one in the background that you would like to include in the plane of focus. Select these points from the scene beforehand, not from the ground-glass image. Keep one hand on the focus adjustment of the rear standard and the other on the tilt adjustment of the front standard. Bring the foreground point into focus and then refocus for the background point. Make a mental note of the amount you had to turn the knob to refocus between them.

equipped, bubble levels are available as an accessory.

4. Select a plane of focus. Make a judgment based on the parts of the scene you would like to appear in focus, and imagine the plane slicing through the scene in a position that will give you that focus with the least possible depth of field. As with the adjustments of the back, lens swing and tilt can be combined so the plane of focus can cut through the subject at any angle. Select the placement of the plane of focus carefully so you can achieve the depth of field you need without having to stop down the lens beyond its sharpest apertures (see *diffraction*, p. 118). Pick three points in your image to define the desired plane of focus. These points will form a triangle to help you visualize the surface of the invisible plane cutting through the image. The farther apart the three points are, the more accurate you can be in isolating that particular

Tilt the lens a few degrees in the direction indicated by the Scheimpflug Principle; for a tabletop plane below camera level, you will need to tilt the top of the lensboard forward. Focus again on the two points, first one then the other. The amount of refocusing needed should diminish. Tilt a little more and then refocus again. As you proceed, the distance between correct focus for the two points will get smaller and smaller until they are both in focus at once. If you find you need to move the focus farther each time, you have passed the correct tilt and are moving away from it.

plane when you adjust the lens plane. If your image allows it, one of your selected points should be in the extreme background and the other two on the extreme left and right of the foreground.

5. Adjust the lens tilt to bring two of your selected points, one near and one far, into focus simultaneously. While you are under the darkcloth viewing the ground-glass image, use one hand to tilt the lens and the other to focus with the rear standard. Before you tilt the front away from zero position, focus on one, then the other, of your selected points. Notice how far you have to move the back to focus from one to the other. Change the angle of the lens slightly in the direction indicated by the Scheimpflug Principle. Adjusting the lens tilt moves the plane of focus away from the vertical around a horizontal axis at right angles to the monorail. Remember, the plane of focus and the lens and film planes will meet in a line. Once

more, focus on one point, then the other again, back and forth, and check to see whether the distance you have had to move the back to focus from one to the other has decreased. If so, the two points are closer to being in focus simultaneously, that is, closer to being in the plane of focus.

Continue to adjust the lens tilt by very small amounts. Focus both points after each adjustment to check that the distance between their focused positions continues to decrease. If it has decreased, you are approaching the lens angle at which the focus position is the same for both points, meaning that both points will lie in the plane of focus.

If you adjust the lens tilt by a small amount and find that you must increase the distance you move the focus adjustment between the two points, you have moved the lens past the correct position, or in the wrong direction. For most photographs, the amount you will have to tilt the lens away from normal position will probably be quite small, so use very tiny adjustments of the angle.

6. Use the lens swing to tip the plane of focus left and right. If your two foreground points require a focus plane slanted from side to side, use the same procedure as above to adjust the lens swing until both points are simultaneously in focus. When you have found the correct position of the lens and they are both in focus, check the near and far points again. Unless your lens has been rotated (with the swing) exactly around its rear nodal point (p. 113), you will probably have to readjust the tilt very slightly. The thickness of your lensboard and lens mount will affect the position of the nodal point, and the design geometry of your particular camera (see the next section) decides the exact axis around which the lens swings.

7. Select the working aperture. Once the plane of focus has been properly positioned, close the diaphragm until you see the desired depth of field in the ground-glass image.

Focusing on the ring in this setup, with the camera in normal position, results in a plane of focus cutting through the image in this position. It is not possible to bring the entire scene into focus by closing down the aperture for depth of field.

Choose three points in the scene to define the position for your plane of focus. They should appear relatively far apart on the ground glass and be sharply defined to make your job of adjusting and focusing easier.

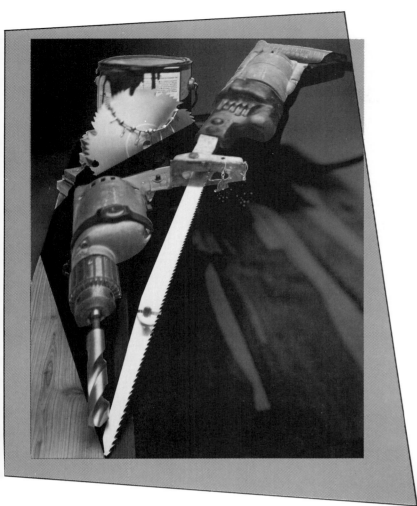

This plane of focus was selected to allow all of the image to be brought into focus with the largest aperture (the minimum depth of field) possible. It required both a tilt and swing of the lens plane. Here, with the lens wide open, it shows the plane of focus cutting through the image.

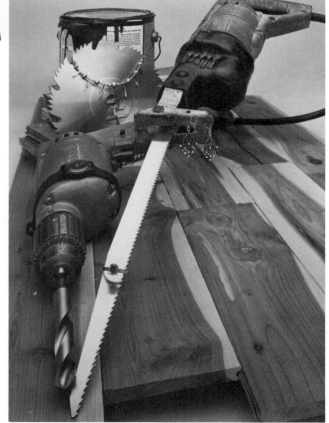

Closing down the lens to a middle aperture created enough depth of field for convincing sharpness in the final image.

Base vs. Axis Tilts

Not all cameras are designed to have the tilt pivot in the same position. Most monorail cameras offer *axis* tilts, meaning the lens and ground-glass tilt around their own centers on a horizontal axis. Some use *base* tilts, in which the front and rear tilts pivot around a horizontal axis at the base of the standard. Current flatbed designs—field, press, and technical cameras—have backs that tilt from the base. Although you can make exactly the same photograph using a camera with either base or axis tilts, this design difference can make some unexpected differences in the operational steps needed to achieve that image.

In cameras having either axis or base tilts, a rise or fall is a movement of the lensboard or back along the upright member of the standard. With axis tilts, the standards themselves are always perpendicular to the rail, but the standards on a base-tilt camera tilt along with the lens or back.

Tilting the lens on a base-tilt camera will move it farther from the film, changing the image distance, and once tilted, a vertical shift will change the image distance once again. Also, tilting the lens at the base moves the lens away from the swing axis. In other words, adding a swing to a base-tilted lens moves the whole lens in a circular path rather than rotating it around the vertical swing axis. Swinging the lens in an arc moves the nodal point of the lens, thereby requiring considerable readjustments of focus and tilt. Axis tilts have the advantage of requiring less refocusing of the image after each movement, but have the disadvantage that an extreme back tilt can block insertion of the film holder.

At least two monorail cameras, Arca and Rajah, include both axis and base tilts. The Sinar P offers a unique system that tilts back and lens around an axis between base and center, using a very sophisticated geometry to simplify the focusing and adjustment process. Although many photographers express strong preferences for one system or camera, the technique of adjusting any of the available cameras will rapidly become second nature with practice.

These two photographs show the results of adding a front rise to a tilted lens with two different cameras. This camera uses axis tilts.

This camera, having base tilts, requires more refocusing after adding one camera movement to another.

Exposure Compensations

Bellows Extension Factor

The only limitation to focusing on close objects with your view camera is the length of your bellows, and you can remove even that limitation by adding an additional standard and another bellows. This freedom to focus on nearby objects is one of the great virtues of the camera, but exercising it introduces you to another important photographic principle. This principle, the *Inverse Square Law*, is ordinarily hidden from users of small cameras by the designers of those cameras.

The illumination available from a light source depends upon the distance from it. Imagine a long, windowless corridor with only one light bulb at one end. The farther from that light bulb you stand, the darker it is where you are and, for example, the harder it would be to read by that light. The film in a view camera is also in a long, win-

dowless corridor, the bellows, and the lens is the light source. *Bellows extension* is the length of that corridor. The more closely you focus, the longer the corridor you make for your film — the greater the bellows extension — and the farther the light is from the film. This means that by decreasing the object distance, the intensity of the light reaching the film is diminished.

Most photographers whose experience is limited to small cameras assume the light intensity reaching the film is only affected by the light level of the scene and by the selected aperture. Within certain limits, this is not a damaging misconception. With any camera, a normal exposure is based upon an infinity focus, at which the lens and film are one focal length apart. Focusing on a closer object moves the film farther from the lens, diminishing the light intensity. In order for the light intensity to be diminished by a noticeable amount, however, the object distance has to be less than about seven times the focal length. Since the focusing mounts for most small camera lenses are intentionally designed to prevent their use at object distances less than seven times their focal length, users of these lenses can produce satisfactory work within the limits of their equipment and in ignorance of bellows extension effects.

Your view camera has no built-in barrier to keep you from focusing more closely than seven times the focal length. If you do, you will reduce the illumination reaching the film plane enough to need to compensate for the light loss. The *bellows extension factor* is the measure of this necessary exposure compensation.

You can calculate the bellows extension factor and multiply the measured (uncompensated) exposure by it, or you can make an educated guess at the needed exposure increase. But in order to do either it is important to know how far the film is from the lens. All your normal exposure calculations are based on an object distance of infinity, the shortest bellows extension possible with a given lens. This is your starting point. At infinity focus, the lens and film are separated by one focal length. With a 300mm lens at infinity focus, the lens and film are about 12 inches apart (remember that 25mm is approximately 1 inch). With this lens, which you might choose for general use on an 8x10 camera, you will need to calculate a bellows extension factor when you focus more closely

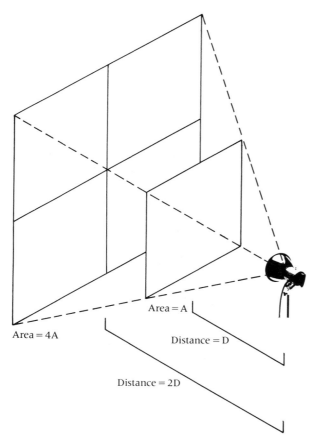

Area = 4A

Area = A

Distance = D

Distance = 2D

The illumination from this lamp that falls on the close card would have to cover a card four times the area if it were twice the distance away. The area for the same illumination increases as the square of the distance.

than about 2 meters, or almost 7 feet. Once you have focused inside this range, measure (or estimate) the actual distance between lens and film.

The *Inverse Square Law* is the principle of physics governing bellows extension and, like other laws of nature, it cannot be ignored without consequence. It tells us that the intensity of a light source diminishes with the square of the distance from it. In our long corridor, if you move twice as far from the bulb, you are illuminated one-fourth as much. At three times the distance, you are illuminated with one-ninth the light. Similarly, if you are using a 150mm lens, and want to make a photograph with the bellows extended to 300mm (12 inches), you will need four times the normal exposure. With the film twice as far from the lens as the infinity focus on which a normal exposure is based, the illumination is diminished to one-fourth normal and the exposure must be increased by a factor of four, or two extra stops.

There are several methods and formulas for calculating the bellows extension factor, and they will all result in the same compensation. The simplest formula is this: the bellows extension factor is equal to the extended bellows length squared, divided by the focal length squared. The indicated exposure (the one determined by metering) should be multiplied (increased) by this factor. You can increase exposure by using a larger aperture or a slower shutter speed.

With most black-and-white work, a careful estimate of the exposure compensation will be sufficient. With color materials, especially reversal film, measurement and calculation will be necessary. Copy work almost always demands compensation for bellows extension because short object distances are common.

Reciprocity Failure

The *Law of Reciprocity* tells us that the correct exposure for a given film in a given lighting situation may equally well be any of several equivalent combinations of aperture (illumination) and shutter speed (time). If we increase the illumination, we may decrease the time by the same amount (and vice versa) without affecting the exposure. Another way of stating this is to say that the film's speed, or *exposure index*, is constant.

Your work with the view camera will eventually introduce you to a characteristic of

This camera is focused at infinity with its 150mm (6-inch) lens.

film rarely noticed by users of small cameras. That is, the Law of Reciprocity is valid only within a limited range of exposure times. *Reciprocity failure*, or the failure of the reciprocity law, is a diminished film speed and increased contrast due to very long or very short exposure times. Most films obey the reciprocity law and have a consistent exposure index only for exposures shorter than 1 second and longer than 1/1000 second. A hand camera is rarely used outside that range. However, because your large-format camera with its longer focal length lenses requires smaller apertures to achieve sufficient depth of field, you will often find yourself making very long exposures. And you will often find yourself having to compensate for the reciprocity failure by making those long exposures even longer.

Compensating for Reciprocity Failure. Accurate compensation tables for each different film's reciprocity characteristics are available from the manufacturer, and are sometimes packaged with the film. Since the degree of reciprocity failure depends on how much light actually gets to the film, you must consider light losses such as filter factors and bellows extension *before* figuring reciprocity compensation. Calculating bellows extension, for example, after reciprocity failure compensation will result in underexposure.

When the camera is focused on a close object, the bellows extension is 10 inches. The formula for bellows extension factor (BEF) is:

$$\frac{(BE)^2}{(FL)^2} = BEF, \text{ where } \begin{array}{l} BE = \text{bellows extension} \\ FL = \text{focal length} \end{array}$$

The factor is 100/36, or about 3. The compensation should be made either by multiplying the exposure time by 3 or by increasing the aperture by about 1½ stops.

In the absence of reciprocity tables, use the following as a rough guide for exposures on black-and-white film. With a metered exposure near 1 second, your film loses half its speed from reciprocity failure and needs one stop more exposure. At an exposure of about 10 seconds, it loses half its speed once again, needing two extra stops. At 100 seconds, film speed is one-eighth normal and needs three extra stops. These exposure compensations *must* be added to your measured exposures or your film will be underexposed. To compensate for the increased contrast that also results from such long exposures, reduce your development time by 10 percent, 20 percent, and 30 percent respectively for the three examples above. These exposure compensations are accurate when increasing the aperture. Giving the film extra exposure time will require slightly more compensation because the film's speed continues to diminish with extended exposure. Three extra stops for a 100-second exposure, which with a constant exposure index would total 800 seconds, should actually be 1200 seconds.

Color film is affected by reciprocity failure more severely than black-and-white film. Not only does the film speed change for long and very short exposures, but it changes a different amount for each of the three color-sensitive layers comprising color film. So reciprocity failure brings a color shift that in many cases cannot be corrected by filtration. Knowing this, film manufacturers make professional color films for different exposure ranges: Kodak's Type S is for short exposures, and Type L is for long.

Exposures shorter than 1/1000 second occur so infrequently for the large-format photographer that you probably needn't be concerned with reciprocity failure in that exposure range. Large, professional strobe lighting equipment usually produces light bursts of longer duration, and the leaf shutters commonly used with large-format lenses rarely have speeds exceeding 1/500 second. If you do encounter very short duration exposures, take the time to test for reciprocity failure with the materials you plan to use before making any important photographs.

You can test your final calculations for exposure, including bellows extension and reciprocity failure, with a sheet of Polaroid film (p. 145). But it is a good practice, and an economical one as well, to avoid using Polaroid tests in place of calculation.

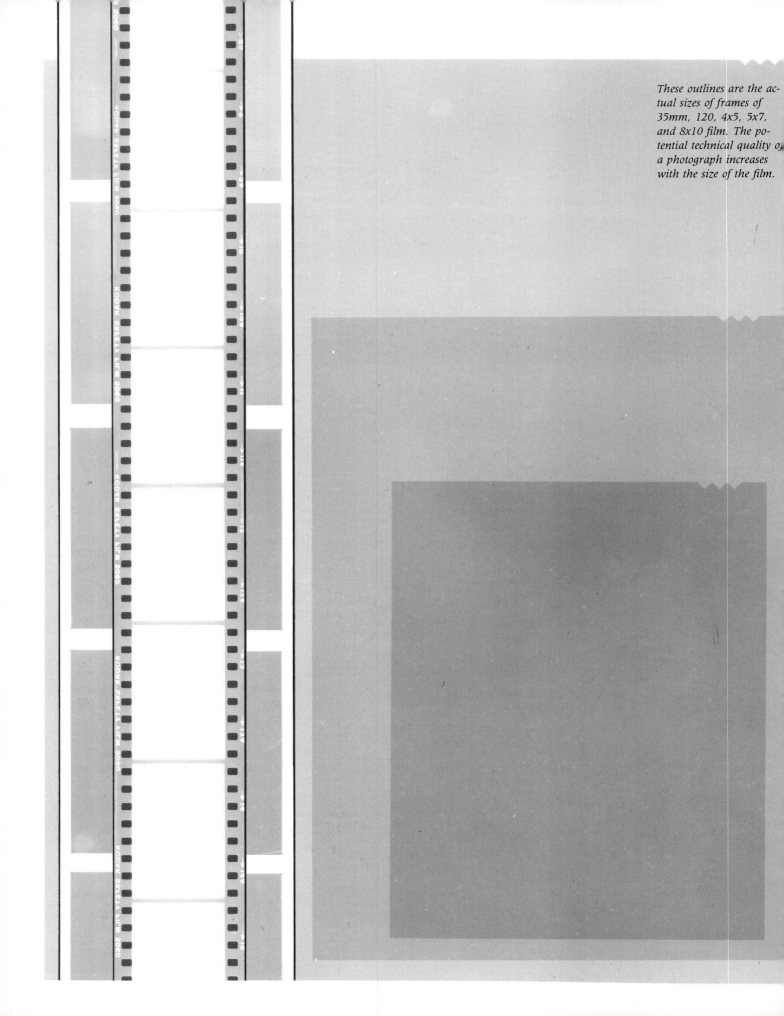

These outlines are the actual sizes of frames of 35mm, 120, 4x5, 5x7, and 8x10 film. The potential technical quality of a photograph increases with the size of the film.

4 Film and Development

One of the major virtues of the view camera is its unique film system. Large-format cameras use film in flat sheets, with dimensions that correspond to the nominal size of the camera. For example, 4-inch by 5-inch sheets are used in a 4x5 camera. Each sheet is loaded, exposed, and processed individually so you will have more steps to follow than with roll film, but you will find that the advantages more than make up for this minor inconvenience.

The Advantages of the Film System

Film in Sheets
The single-sheet film system used for view cameras gives you more freedom than any other system to shift from one kind of film to another. Once set up, many commercial shots are photographed first on Polaroid, then successively on black-and-white, color negative, and color reversal film. Each use for the photograph can then be satisfied with no sacrifice in quality: color transparency to the printer for a brochure, black-and-white prints from a negative for a press release, and color prints from a negative for the office walls.

A Variety of Film
Kodak lists dozens of different emulsions available in sheet-film sizes, more different types of film than are available in rolls. These include special-purpose films for scientific, graphic arts, and aerial photography. Many of the available films are not only useful to their intended fields but also provide raw material for the experiments of inventive artists.

Large Film
Another advantage of large-format film, obvious to anyone who has ever seen a print made from a large negative, is the sheer visual quality that results from the great expanse of film. Sharpness, resolution, and graininess, common indicators of image quality in a photograph, are all related to the degree of enlargement from negative to print. A 35mm negative has less than 9 cm^2 of image

area and a 6x6cm negative from 120 film has 36 cm^2. A 4x5 negative (10 by 12cm), however, yields 120 cm^2 of image. These figures mean that, all other things being equal, a print having the same fineness of detail can be made more than thirteen times larger from a 4x5 negative than a 35mm negative. Or, if the same size print is made from both, the resolution, sharpness, and granularity will be many times better from the larger negative. Larger film sizes, such as 8x10, are most often printed by contact for the highest possible image quality. Many artists have elected to work solely with 8x10 for this reason alone.

For the advertising photographer, sheet film is often necessary when a client's needs include retouching. Concepts impossible to express by photographic means are made visible at the hands of an experienced retoucher, who asks only to be supplied with a transparency large enough to work on directly.

Separate Development
The Zone System, an advanced technique for black-and-white photography, uses controlled exposure and development as a way of adjusting the contrast of a negative, and can be used effectively only if development can be varied from one negative to the next. Once you are comfortable with the camera and can begin to explore its expressive uses, study the Zone System to introduce complete tonal control to your black-and-white picture-making. Several good texts are available on the subject.

Sheet Film Storage

Sheet film, sometimes called *cut film*, may be purchased in boxes that ordinarily contain either 25 or 100 sheets (for black-and-white; color film comes in 10- or 50-sheet boxes). Start with a small box: you will find the box itself useful to store and transport small quantities of film after you have exposed all the film in it. The film is contained in a sealed foil package of 25 sheets; 100-sheet boxes contain four foil packs.

Unless you expect to use all the film soon after you purchase it, keep large boxes refrigerated or frozen to preserve the film and transfer one pack at a time to a smaller box as you need it. To avoid condensation on the film's surface, allow the cold film to reach room temperature before opening the packet. Give refrigerated film at least 1 hour, and frozen film 4 hours, to reach room temperature. Sealed foil packs are airtight. If you wish to refrigerate an opened pack, reseal the box in a plastic bag first, preferably on a dry day.

The film is packed inside a box made of three nested lids to prevent light leaks. Store your empty boxes (*only* your empty boxes) with the outer two lids nested in the same direction (see illustration). This keeps out dust, and a glance at the bottom of the box will allow you to tell by the visible edges of the center lid around the bottom of the inner lid that the box is empty.

Sheet film is sold in three-part boxes, nested to assure lightproof storage.

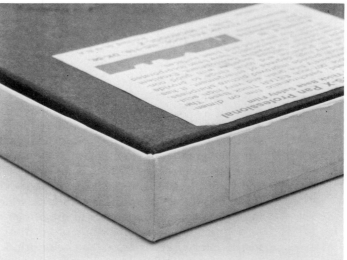

Loading the Film

The Film Holder
Sheet film is sold as raw stock. Before you can expose the film in your camera, you must load it into a reusable lighttight *film holder*, which is inserted for the exposure into the camera's spring back. To develop the exposed film, you must remove it from the holder. Since the film you are most likely to use is either color or panchromatic black-and-white, you will be loading and unloading film holders in complete darkness.

The standard film holder for sheet film is a *double* sheet-film holder. This holder provides space for two sheets of film, and has two identical faces each with a shallow compartment to hold the film. Each face has a hinged flap at the bottom to facilitate film insertion and has its own separate *darkslide*, a flat, opaque plastic sheet that slides through a felt-lined slot at the top of the holder and down in tracks along the sides of the film compartment to seat into the flap and cover the film. When the shallow film compartment is covered by the darkslide, the film inside is protected from the light.

After the film holder has been inserted properly into the camera's spring back, the darkslide must be withdrawn before the exposure is made. The black felt in the slot acts as a light trap to block light from fogging the film when the darkslide is withdrawn. Other styles of film holders that may better suit

When the bottom of a film box shows only one rim, the third part of the box is nested inside. Do not open it in the light.

If you store empty film boxes nested this way, the dust will be kept out and you can tell them apart from the boxes containing film.

This is a standard double sheet-film holder for 4x5 film. One of its two supplied darkslides is withdrawn, revealing the compartment for one sheet of film.

your purposes are described on p. 141, along with more detail on this standard holder.

The Darkslide

When you are photographing you will want to have several holders with you, since each holds only enough film for two exposures. The film holders are all identical, and each has two identical faces, so you will need a foolproof system to avoid exposing the same sheet of film twice. In most film-holding systems for large-format cameras there is a darkslide to prevent unwanted exposure when the holder is out of the camera. For standard double sheet-film holders, the darkslide performs an additional task — it gives you a way to tell whether the sheet of film it covers has been exposed.

The top rim (or handle) of the darkslide is black on one side, and white (or polished metal) on the other. Run your finger along the white side and feel the short row of bumps or holes. The black side is smooth. These distinctions of color and texture allow you to indicate to yourself whether the film inside the holder has been exposed. White side out indicates unexposed film; black means exposed film or an empty holder. Before you insert a film holder for exposure, make sure the darkslide has its white rim out. When you replace the darkslide into the holder after exposing the film, leave the black side out. When loading or unloading holders, use the bumps on the white side for fingertip identification in the dark.

The white edge of the darkslide, signifying unexposed film, has bumps for identification in the dark. The black side is smooth. On each side of the holder's top there is a small wire clip to prevent inadvertent removal of the darkslide.

Film Code Notches

Since only one side of the film is coated with a light-sensitive emulsion to receive an exposure, you must load the film holder so that the emulsion side of each sheet will face the lens when inserted into the camera's spring back. Because you will be loading holders in the dark, some nonvisual means of identifying the emulsion side is necessary.

Film manufacturers cut *code notches* into the corner of each sheet for identification in the dark. To locate the emulsion side, hold the film sheet by its edges in a vertical position, like a page to be read. Feel the perimeter of the film for the pattern of cut notches. When the notches are in the upper right or lower left corner of a sheet held vertically, the emulsion side of the film is facing you. Slide the film into the holder with that side facing out, to be covered by the darkslide.

The notches also identify the type of film. Each different sheet-film emulsion for use in a camera bears a different pattern of notches. Graphic arts sheet films and others that can be handled in safelight are not notched. Film manufacturers publish diagrams of the code notch patterns for all their films along with other film data in pamphlets or books; the notch code for the film in a box is also usually depicted on the film box label or in the instructions packed with it. If you need to identify the type of a sheet of film, for example, if you have gotten two unmarked holders mixed up, use a pencil to trace the outline of the notches onto paper while in the dark. After you put the film away, you can match the code to the manufacturer's diagram. Once you learn a film's notch code, your fingertips will be able to identify the film immediately. Because of the way the notches are cut into a stack of film during manufacture, they may not always be the same depth, but the shape and spacing will be the same.

How to Load Film

In your darkroom, prepare a very clean work surface free of clutter. To be comfortable you will need at least a meter's width of counter, with nothing nearby to knock over. Wash your hands thoroughly with soap and water and dry them completely. Any fingerprints you get on the film during loading will appear as permanent marks during development. Have only the box of unexposed film and the empty holders in front of you. If your darkroom is warm, keep a clean towel

Each sheet of film has code notches in one corner that indicate the type of emulsion and the side on which it is coated.

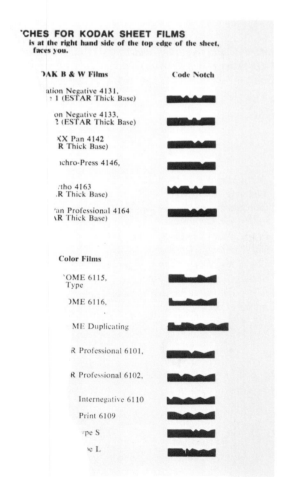

The code notches are your clue to which emulsion is on the film as well as which side of the sheet it is on. Each film manufacturer publishes a list of code notches for identification.

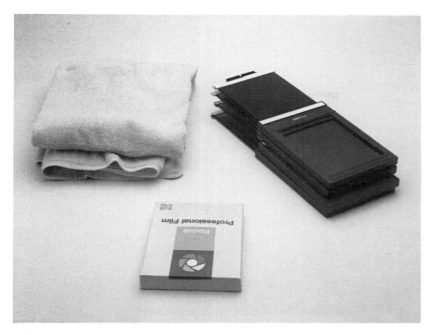

Make sure your counter is clean and uncluttered before you try to load film there in the dark. Have your film and holders ready, and keep a towel nearby to clean and dry your hands.

Lay the stack of film across the box it came in with the emulsion side down so it will be easy to find in the dark and stay dust-free.

nearby to wipe perspiration from your hands. Withdraw the darkslides almost all the way, and leave the white side facing out. Dust the holders using a vacuum cleaner, compressed air, or a clean camel's hair brush and stack them to one side.

Before attempting to load any film you expect to use for a photograph, practice loading your film holder in the light with a piece of scrap film. You may wish to begin with a small box of Tri-X Ortho, a black-and-white sheet film you can load and develop under a 1A (dark red) safelight. This practice will make your transition to working with sheet film more gentle.

Turn off the light and, if working in an unfamiliar darkroom, wait a few minutes to allow your pupils to dilate so you can make sure there is no light leaking into the room. Phosphorescent clock and timer dials, or even the afterglow of some fluorescent lights, can fog film if they are near enough.

Open the film box and nest the three sections in an open position. Remove the foil pack containing the film, tear it open, and remove the film in a stack, holding it only by its edges. Set aside any paper cover sheets and lay the pack of film sideways across the open box, emulsion side down. This way the film will be easy to find and dust won't settle on the emulsion side of the film while you work.

Handling it by the edges, remove one sheet of film from the top of the stack. *Do not touch the emulsion side,* and touch the back of the film only if necessary. Flip the sheet so that the code notches are in the upper right-hand corner; the emulsion side will be facing you. Pull down the bottom flap on the holder to reveal the tracks or channel for the film. With 4x5 film, you can hold the film holder in one hand and the film in the other. Larger sizes will probably require you to leave the holder on the counter and hold the film with both hands. Slide the film in and up to the top of the holder. Run a fingernail lightly along the track above the film on each side to make sure you haven't gotten it in the track for the darkslide instead. Remember that the code notches must be in the upper right or lower left corner of the holder so that the emulsion side will face the lens during exposure. With the film in its proper position at the very top of the holder, the flap will close easily. Dust the emulsion surface of the film with a camel's hair brush or compressed air. Slide the darkslide into its closed position; if it seems difficult to close, you may have the film in the wrong track.

Load a sheet of film in the other side of the holder in the same way, load the rest of your stack of holders, and enclose the remaining film in its box before turning on the lights. There is probably no advantage to first returning the film to its foil pack, but many photographers do so. Store and transport the film holders in plastic bags to keep out dust.

If you do not have access to a darkroom, you can load and unload your holders in a *changing bag* made from an opaque cloth. These bags are available from most camera stores, but they are constricting and uncomfortable, and will probably create severe dust problems.

Exposing the Film

Sheet film is no different from roll film during exposure. Your method of determining the correct exposure will be the same. You will probably use a light meter (p. 138). Make sure you have read and understood the section on exposure compensations (p. 55). The film holder fits into the spring back to form a lighttight seal with the camera body, and you need to withdraw the darkslide (p. 61) for the exposure and return it (black side out) before removing the holder from the back.

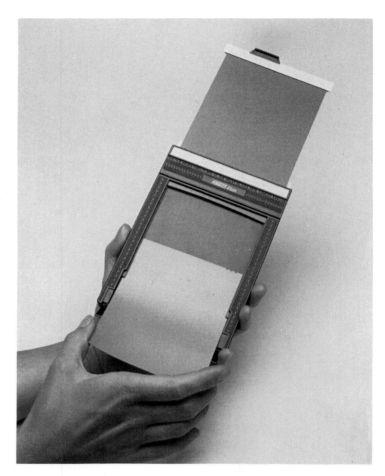

Holding the film by its edges, slide it into the correct slots at the sides of the compartment in the holder. The emulsion is correctly facing out when the code notches are in the upper right or lower left corner of a vertical film sheet.

Developing the Film

As you might have imagined, the development of sheet film differs somewhat from that of roll film. The chemical process itself is the same for any size or shape of a specific film, but the procedure for immersing and agitating large-format film in development chemicals will be new to you.

As with any other film format, proper processing of sheet film requires that you: 1. Use the necessary solutions in correct sequence and at a controlled temperature; 2. Agitate the film or solution to promote the same rate of chemical activity over the entire film surface; 3. Wash away all residual chemicals; and 4. Protect the film from extraneous light and physical damage. Several methods of processing will satisfy all of these requirements, and your choice of one will be affected by the kind and quantity of film you use as well as by your equipment and working environment.

The Custom Lab and Quantity Processing

Users of large-format film, particularly color film, often choose to have it processed at a *custom lab*. These commercial darkrooms primarily serve professional photographers, and have a large-scale manual or automated film processing setup called a *line*. Named for the linear progression of solutions and for Kodak's brand name of processing chemicals, an E-6 line is for *color reversal* films (positive transparencies, often called *chromes*) and a C-41 line is for color negatives. Most labs also have a black-and-white line.

Color film processing is economical and easily controlled only with large batch processing, and only a large-volume studio can justify in-house color development. A discussion of the methods used in processing large quantities of film is beyond the scope of this book, but information on these methods can be readily obtained from retailers serving industrial photographic accounts and from the manufacturers of processing chemicals and equipment.

Small-Volume Methods

Three methods, each based upon a different container, are used for processing small

quantities of sheet film: tray development, open tanks with hangers, and closed tanks. At least one of these methods will suit your working habits. The development procedures in this chapter are all tailored for black-and-white film, but may be readily adapted to color. If you expect to develop color film, remember that color chemicals pose a much greater health hazard and require better darkroom ventilation and skin protection. Since most color processes require solutions to be much warmer than ambient (room) temperature, it is more difficult to maintain the chemicals at a constant temperature. Maintaining the temperature of the warmer solution is made even more difficult by introducing room-temperature objects such as film and hangers into it. Since small variations in temperature will produce more noticeable changes in color film than in black-and-white, you will have to pay much greater attention to controlling the temperature when developing color film.

Tray Development

If you already have a working small-format darkroom, you can develop your first sheets of film in your print-processing trays. The technique is much the same as that for developing prints, and you will need no additional equipment. The room must be lighttight, of course, as the film will be in an open tray for several minutes. Even a slight light leak can spoil your results with fog.

Setting Up. Use trays at least one standard size larger than your film: 5x7 trays for 4x5 film, 11x14 trays for 8x10. Until you are experienced in tray development, you will probably be more comfortable with trays two sizes larger than your film. Lay out five trays in the sink so that you can easily find them in the dark and determine which is the first in the sequence. The first tray should be plain water at the same temperature as the developer, followed by trays containing the developer, stop bath, and fixer, and a final tray of water.

Of the three methods used for processing small quantities of sheet film, tray development will allow you to use the minimum amounts of chemicals. Depending upon the capacity of your chosen film developer, you can use as little as 75ml per sheet of 4x5 film (20 square inches), or 300ml per sheet of

8x10 (four times the area). The solution in the tray must be deep enough to allow your hands some freedom of movement below the surface. You will want to practice developing some scrap film to learn how much solution you will need.

The agitation procedure for developing more than one sheet at a time requires you to touch the film constantly during processing. The gelatin emulsion is extremely soft and fragile when wet and you must exercise caution throughout the process to avoid damaging it. Short fingernails and extreme vigilance are advisable. Also, your hands will be immersed in the processing chemicals, so if your skin is sensitive to photographic chemicals, wear surgical gloves. The thinner the gloves, the better; your tactile sense is your only guide in the dark.

The presence of your hands in the developer will change its temperature. Using stainless steel or enamel trays for your chemicals and surrounding them with a water bath will help keep the temperatures constant. If you don't use a water bath, measure the temperature of the developer after processing your first test sheets to determine any change. If the temperature has increased, you may need to decrease your development time slightly to compensate. Try using the time from the film's developer/time/temperature chart that corresponds to a temperature halfway between your beginning and ending temperatures. You should also set your stop bath and fixer at the higher temperature to prevent minor reticulation, a surface effect of temperature change on the film that resembles increased graininess.

Agitation and Processing. After your trays have been set up, make sure your hands are clean and dry before turning off the lights and removing the exposed film from your holders or storage box. Make a stack of all the sheets you plan to develop and hold the stack by the edges in one hand. With the other hand place the sheets one at a time, emulsion side up, in the first tray — a water presoak. Wait for each sheet to sink below the surface before adding the next. From the time you place the sheets in water until they are hung up to dry, they should be kept moving. If you allow one sheet to settle on another in the tray for very long, even in water, the edge of one sheet can leave a permanent mark on the other.

A water presoak of a minute or longer with agitation will prevent *air bells*, the circu-

Hold the stack of film sheets in your left hand, keeping them under the surface of the liquid but not resting on the bottom of the tray.

With your right thumb, gently separate the bottom sheet from the rest by peeling it down slightly.

Slide the bottom sheet out from under the stack. Make sure you don't scrape it on the corner of the stack on the way out.

Place the sheet on top of the stack, taking care not to scratch the sheet directly below it with a corner.

Gently push the stack down to submerge all the sheets, then begin the process again with the bottom sheet.

Drain the stack by one corner before transferring it to the next solution. Always hold the film by the edges when possible.

lar marks caused by bubbles clinging to the film during development. It will also give you time to ensure that none of the sheets have stuck together. If you inadvertently place two sheets in the tray simultaneously, they will indeed stick together. In the developer, this is a catastrophe; in the presoak, merely an annoyance. Slowly peel the two apart, holding them underwater and taking care not to scratch other sheets in the tray.

The agitation procedure for sheet film in a tray (shown in the illustrations on this page) requires the constant repetition of a series of motions cycling each sheet through the stack from top to bottom. The corners of one sheet, as well as your fingernails, can scratch the soft emulsion on another sheet. Preventing scratches in the film's emulsion is easier when you process fewer sheets and have deeper solutions in the trays. Practice developing four sheets of film in trays at least half full. After you become proficient with four, you will be able to increase the number of sheets you can develop at one time without damage. Although it is possible to achieve satisfactory results with more, eight sheets is a comfortable maximum for most people.

Once the film sheets are all in the presoak, gently arrange them into a stack with the emulsion side up. Keep the stack off the tray bottom by holding the fingers of one hand, palm up, under the film. If you are right-handed, you will probably use your left hand for this. For the rest of the process, handle the film only by the bottom (the backing side) and edges.

With the fingers of your left hand under the stack of film, separate the bottom sheet from the rest by pulling down one corner with your right thumb. Carefully slide the sheet out, lift it out of the solution, and replace it on top of the stack. Push the whole stack down gently with your right palm to immerse the top sheet. Repeat this procedure every 3 to 5 seconds for the duration of the 1-minute presoak. At the end of the minute, lift the stack of film out of the water tray and drain it for a few seconds. Place it in the developer, start the timer, and begin the agitation cycle again.

While the film is in the developer, the warmth and extra agitation generated by your fingers in handling the film can be a source of uneven development. Rotate the stack or the entire tray 90° each minute of development so that you handle each corner instead of just one. The more sheets you develop at once, the higher the risk of uneven development; keeping the film in a stack prevents fresh developer from reaching the center of each sheet until it comes around for agitation.

Ten seconds before the correct development time is over, remove the stack of film by the edges and drain by one corner. Place the stack into the stop bath and agitate in the same pattern as you used in the developer. Drain again, transfer to the fixer, and agitate in the fixer for the appropriate time. After fixing, the film will need to be washed.

Washing and Drying. If you wish to wash the film in trays, transfer the stack to a tray of fresh water at the same temperature as the developing solutions. One sheet at a time, transfer the film to a second tray of water. Empty the first tray, refill it with water, and transfer the film back to the first tray one sheet at a time. Empty the second tray, refill, and repeat this sequence for the duration of the wash time. Other methods used to wash sheet film are described later in this chapter.

In a tray, soak the washed film in a wetting agent, such as Photo-flo, mixed with distilled water. Using distilled water with the wetting agent will help prevent water spots. Then hang each sheet by one corner from a

clip or clothespin to dry in a dust-free place. Do not use a squeegee on the film to remove excess wetting agent; it can easily damage the film and its use is unnecessary.

Tank Development
If you wish to keep your hands out of the chemicals entirely, consider using the tanks-and-hangers method. The extra equipment you will need includes *sheet-film hangers* and *sheet-film developing tanks*.

A hanger is a stainless steel or plastic frame designed to hold the film by its edges. Different sizes of hangers are available to hold each of the standard film sizes (4x5,

With sheet-film hangers, you can develop film without handling it and without having your hands in chemicals. The empty hanger shows its loading clip in the open position.

After washing and then a rinse in a wetting agent, hang each sheet by one corner to dry in a dust-free place.

Hangers and tanks are made for each common size of sheet film. Most are stainless steel. The large hangers hold four sheets of 4x5 film and fit a tank made for 8x10.

Hold and carry hangers between your hands. Be careful not to scratch the film with a hanger's sharp corner.

To agitate the film, lift the hangers out of the tank slowly and drain them for a few seconds in this position before returning them slowly into the tank. Then repeat the action, draining them to the other side.

5x7, and 8x10) and to fit inside the readily available sheet-film developing tanks. Hangers that fit 8x10 tanks and hold four sheets of 4x5 film are also available. Each frame has a handle that allows you to agitate and transport the sheets. The handle on each hanger frame is a bar that fits across the top of the tank; the film hangs suspended from the handle into the tank. Since you must fill each tank with enough liquid to immerse the entire sheet, you will use considerably more of each chemical than you will with the tray method.

Sheet-film developing tanks are made of stainless steel, hard rubber, or plastic in sizes corresponding to the hanger sizes. You can also buy water-jacketed stainless steel tanks that use a constant flow of tempered water for precise control of processing temperatures. Tanks are made to accommodate only a certain number of hangers; the smallest tanks hold a maximum of six, larger ones hold up to twelve. As you will see when you try tank development, the size of your hands may be the limiting factor on how many sheets you can develop at once.

Tanks are available with airtight tops or with lids that float on the surface of the chemical to reduce its contact with the air. Covering the tank slows evaporation and oxidation (which spoils developers). If you use a developer that can be replenished after each use and if you keep it from oxidizing, you will not need to prepare developer before each processing session. The developer (and the other chemicals) can be left in the tank for storage. If you expect to develop film frequently, tanks-and-hangers processing allows you to have all the chemicals ready for immediate use at any time.

Setting Up. For tank development, you will need one empty tank in addition to the four — presoak, developer, stop bath, and fixer — for processing. Begin by filling the tanks with your processing chemicals at the correct temperature and setting them out in order. The dry, empty tank should be on the counter next to your empty hangers and the film holders containing the exposed film.

Once the tanks are filled and everything is in place, turn off the light and load the hangers in the dark. One at a time, pry back the covering clip on the hanger, slip the sheet into the frame of the hanger, cover it with the clip, and place the loaded hanger in the dry tank (or in a rack designed for the purpose). When all are loaded properly, lift them out by supporting the protruding ends of the handles along your index fingers, palms facing each other, and lower them carefully into the first tank. Because the film sheets won't stick together, a water presoak is not as important here as it is in tray processing, but a presoak with occasional agitation may still be used to prevent air bells and promote even development.

Agitation and Processing. Agitate the film by lifting all the hangers simultaneously, supporting the handles along the sides of your index fingers. Slowly lift and tilt the hangers to one side until all of the film sheets are out of the solution and draining from one corner. Slowly lower them back into the solution again and repeat the lifting and tilting motion, tilting to the opposite side. This operation of two lift-and-tilt cycles should take not less than 15 seconds. It should be repeated continuously for the first minute and once during each remaining minute of development. Moving the film too rapidly during agitation will produce uneven development at the film's edges. Too little agitation can streak the film (the streaks are called *bromide drag*), although this is a much less common problem. Use this agitation pattern and your standard times for the stop bath and fixer.

Washing and Drying. Wash the film with water by repeatedly filling and emptying the tank, or use one of the specially designed sheet-film washers. Many of the vertical print washers on the market can be used for film in hangers if you remove the interior dividers.

After immersing the film in a wetting agent, hang the film to dry and thoroughly rinse the film hangers and tanks with plain water. Wetting agent allowed to dry on the hangers can affect the results of the next batch of film by accelerating development at the film's edges.

Daylight Developing Tanks

If your darkroom will not accommodate tray or tank processing, if you are processing film while traveling, or if you have a strong aversion to working in darkness (and insist on processing your own sheet film), you may use one of the several closed-tank systems available for sheet film.

Similar to roll-film developing systems, these *daylight tanks* allow liquids to be poured in and out through a light trap, and total darkness is needed only for loading them with film. Usually made for 4x5 and smaller

sheet film, most daylight tanks will hold a maximum of six or eight sheets. For 8x10 sheet film, you can use a daylight processing drum made for color print processing to develop one sheet at a time.

Because each daylight developing tank has its own system for holding the film in place, each requires a different procedure for loading, and all tanks come with directions. Some manufacturers make and recommend accessory loading devices to make the job easier. Except for adjusting the time in the developer slightly to compensate for the different agitation pattern, your normal se-

Special-purpose film washers like this one provide a thorough washing to untended film left in them in hangers.

This daylight tank contains two reels, each with a capacity of six sheets of 4x5 film. It can be agitated by a mechanized roller base. The optional loading platform simplifies this tricky procedure.

quence of chemicals and times will be correct for daylight tank development.

Intermittent agitation during development in a closed tank is likely to result in uneven development, despite the claims of the tank's manufacturer. For the most even development possible with any closed-tank system, fill the tank halfway and agitate it vigorously, constantly, and in a random pattern, including complete inversion. Using a full tank and an agitation pattern similar to that for roll-film tanks, agitating for 5 seconds each minute, you will get results with slightly finer grain, but will risk streaks or

Your negatives will be protected from most environmental damage if kept inside polyethylene or polyester sleeves inside boxes made of acid-free cardboard or polypropylene. Keeping the boxes inside polyethylene bags will further protect the negatives against accidental spills or leaks. In the foreground above is a Mylar sleeve with its acid-free paper envelope. These sleeves provide the safest, most inert surrounding for film.

overdevelopment at the film edges. The instruction sheet packaged with the film will give you development times for trays using constant agitation and for tank development with agitation at one-minute intervals. The time for constant agitation in a tank will be slightly less than that for tray development. Make sure you run tests before developing any important film.

You can wash film in the tank by repeatedly filling it with water and emptying it, or you can remove the film to wash it using any of the methods previously mentioned.

Storing Negatives

Once your processed film is dry, transfer it to a safe package for storage and preservation. Negatives must be protected from heat, humidity, physical damage, and airborne pollutants, particularly sulfur compounds. For the most permanent, or *archival*, storage, only inert plastics such as polyethylene and polyester should touch the film. Currently, the safest material for negative storage is uncoated polyester (Mylar) with a frosted surface.

Special transparent polyethylene storage pages are made to accommodate sheet film in standard sizes. Punched to fit a three-ring binder, each page holds four 4x5 negatives, two 5x7 sheets, or one 8x10. Because the storage sheets are so pliable, a flat box is probably a more suitable container for these pages than a three-ring binder. Negatives stored in transparent polyethylene can be damaged by *ferrotyping*, the tendency for gelatin to conform to a surface in contact with it. Under very humid conditions and some pressure, negatives in polyethylene pages can develop glossy areas from touching the plastic, so don't stack too many sheets together in a box. Acid-free paper envelopes and folders may be a satisfactory option, although those made acid-free by buffering are of questionable long-term value, and sliding negatives in and out of a paper sleeve may cause physical damage. Never use glassine (a translucent paper) or ordinary paper for long-term storage.

Printing

After seeing the prints from your first large-format negatives, you will wonder why anyone would use roll film. All the benchmarks of photographic quality — resolution, detail, sharpness, and fine grain — are the visual evidence of your chosen camera. And elaborate enlarging equipment is unnecessary because the negatives themselves are large; Edward Weston's finest prints were made in a simple contact frame under an ordinary light bulb.

Large-format cameras flourished in the nineteenth century when all prints were made by *contact*: placing the negative in direct contact with a sheet of paper to make a positive image on the paper the same size as the negative. The larger the negative, the larger the print. Enlarging reduces quality by spreading the visual information from a negative over a greater area. The greater the degree of enlargement, the lower the image quality. But a print made by contact is faithful to the negative, retaining all the possible delicacy of tone and crispness of edge.

As a user of a large-format camera, you have the best of both worlds. You can contact-print your negatives for the highest quality, or enlarge them to any size with a lesser degree of enlargement (therefore less quality loss) than with any smaller format. Other than the large size of the negative, all aspects of the printing procedure are identical to those of printing smaller film.

Printing by Contact

In addition to a conventional workspace — darkroom with safelight, trays, and chemicals — all you will need for printing by contact is a sheet of glass and a light source that can be turned on and off to make a correct exposure.

Holding the negative in close contact with the paper is as simple as covering the two, emulsion sides facing, with glass; the weight of a sheet of plate glass slightly larger than the paper should be sufficient. To avoid undesirable marks on the final print, make sure your glass is free of scratches, blemishes, and dust. Occasionally, usually with very thin or very large negatives, some areas of the resulting print will be unsharp from uneven pressure. If this happens, use a thin sheet of foam rubber under the paper, or use a *contact-printing frame*. This simple frame holds a sheet of glass and a backing board (and between them the negative and paper) together with pressure from springs.

Almost any light source will suffice for contact printing. The overhead light in your darkroom, a desk lamp, or even a match can be used, but an enlarger is ideal since it was designed to distribute light very evenly and can be switched on and off accurately with a timer.

Printing by contact allows you to use a broader range of materials on which to print.

A contact-printing frame will hold your negative in close contact with the print material.

This 4x5 negative carrier grips the negative by two sides and stretches it flat for exposure. Larger negatives, particularly ones on thin plastic bases, can swell and buckle from heat during exposure, creating unsharp enlargements.

An enlarger is an ideal light source for contact printing. The light is adjustable and even, and your timer will allow precise and repeatable exposures.

With a large negative and a brighter light source, you can use slow, rich-toned silver chloride printing-out papers or any of the early printing materials such as platinum, gum bichromate, or cyanotype. These printing materials need exposures to light as bright as the sun and rich in ultraviolet, such as a carbon arc or sunlamp, so an enlarger cannot be used. The amount of light that is safe to use in an enlarger is limited because the negative must be close to the source of light (therefore close to the source of heat). A bright enough enlarger light to expose these slow materials would produce too much heat too close to the fragile negative and burn it.

Enlarging

Most professional enlargers will accommodate film sizes up to and including 4x5. An enlarger designed to produce even illumination and to be sturdy enough for 4x5 film will also usually be more satisfactory for smaller negatives than a smaller enlarger. Because most professionals today use either 4x5 or 8x10, enlargers capable of handling a 5x7 sheet have become uncommon. An 8x10 enlarger is as much an investment as buying a new car, and much more difficult to move.

Most enlargers for film sizes larger than 4x5 have a *diffusion* light source, named for the sheet of opal glass or translucent plastic immediately above the negative that provides even illumination by diffusing the light falling on it from above. The alternative, a *condenser* light source, uses a set of lenses above the negative stage to concentrate the light and project it straight down.

A diffusion light source will produce an image of lower contrast than that of a condenser, and spots on the print from dust and surface defects are greatly diminished. This is a great advantage since the glass-sandwich negative holder that is often necessary to hold a large negative flat during printing adds four dust-collecting surfaces to the two on your film. Some diffusion enlargers use fluorescent tubes instead of incandescent bulbs and are called *cold-light* enlargers. A cold-light source prevents problems due to heat, notably buckling or *popping* of the negative during exposure, but the limited output spectrum of the light can interfere with the effective use of variable-contrast or color enlarging papers.

5 Lenses and Shutters

Selecting a lens, or a set of lenses, for your view camera requires more care and knowledge than for any smaller-format camera. Large-format lenses are among the most expensive objects in any photographer's studio, and the array of possible choices can be intimidating, but it is just this variety that makes the view camera an ideal professional tool.

If you are already a serious user of smaller cameras, it will seem strange to you that none of the manufacturers of large-format cameras also makes lenses. When you buy a 35mm "system" camera, you naturally choose from lenses of the same brand. You are assured there will be no mismatch mechanically, optically, or nowadays, electronically. There are no such guarantees with a large-format system.

It is possible, and in fact common, to use one lens for both a 4x5 and an 8x10 camera, or on a press camera one day and on a monorail the next. It is also possible for another lens to work properly for 4x5 and be almost useless for 8x10. Also, unfortunately, a lens that is suitable for one photographer working with 4x5 may not be satisfactory for another photographer using the same equipment.

Basically, you can mount any lens on your camera by having a hole of the correct diameter drilled in a relatively inexpensive lensboard and threading on a retaining ring. Having a lens mounted correctly, however, does not mean it is the correct lens. To determine the correct lens, you must know your own needs and have a general understanding of the characteristics of lenses.

Information about lenses can fill volumes, most of it incidental to their actual use. This chapter includes everything you will need to know about optics to make photographs with a view camera. When you have read and digested this information, and are comfortable with the terminology, read Chapter 7. In it you will find a more in-depth treatment of the design and history of lenses. Many lenses made before you were born are perfectly useful today, and are bar-

gains as well. You will want to make an informed decision when buying a lens, and since many of the lenses made since the turn of the century may be included in your possible choices, the more you know the less money you may have to spend.

Coverage

Before learning anything further about lenses, you will need to be familiar with the term *coverage*. All lenses project a cone of light. When this cone is intercepted by a flat surface, such as film, it forms a circle. To be useful, this circular image must be large enough to "cover" the film size you are using. A lens for a 35mm camera must project a circle large enough to fit around the 24x36mm frame. The smallest circle that will cover 35mm film has a diameter the same as

The array of lenses you can use on a view camera is wider than for any other kind of camera, but you must know more about them than just how to mount one on the camera.

Because of its fixed position in relationship to the film, the lens of a 35mm camera need only just cover the rectangular frame.

The minimum covering circle for a lens for 35mm has a diameter of 43mm.

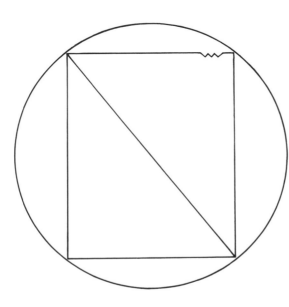

Your lens must project a circle with a diameter at least the size of the film's diagonal to cover the film. For 4x5, that diagonal is 155mm.

the frame diagonal, about 43mm. In order to photograph onto 35mm film, then, a lens must have a *covering circle* (or *circle of coverage*) with a diameter of at least 43mm and must be mounted so that its center, or optical axis, is lined up with the center of the film frame. This lens position is assured by the design of fixed-body cameras like the 35mm SLR. Your view camera, however, offers no such guarantee.

In Chapter 3 we found that one of the virtues of the view camera is that its movements allow the user to move the film away from the optical axis. With a lens like the one described above, having a covering circle just fitting around the frame, any camera movement would cause the image to fall off the film's edge. That is, the projected image would fail to "cover" the film. If you wish to take advantage of your view camera's movements, you need a lens with a covering circle larger than the film. The more extreme the movements, the larger an image circle you need. The size of the circle of coverage is affected by aperture, lens design, image distance, and focal length, all discussed below.

Circle of Good Definition

The circle of coverage of a lens can be defined in two ways. The *circle of illumination* is the entire circular image with edges defined by a sharp cutoff of light caused mostly by vignetting (or shading by the opaque parts of the lens). The *circle of good definition* is the useful part of the projected field of a lens. It is concentric within the circle of illumination — smaller and less obviously defined. Although the circle of illumination can be considered a covering circle, most measurements equate the circle of good definition with the circle of coverage because only inside the circle of good definition does an image have sufficient *resolution* to be considered useful. Resolution is a measure of optical quality based on the ability of a lens to distinguish two small, close-together points from a single point (if you wear eyeglasses, chances are it is to increase the resolution of your eyes). For our purposes, we will use the term circle of coverage to mean the circle of good definition.

Aperture and Coverage

Most lenses project their highest resolution in the center, with the image quality deteriorating as it moves toward the edges. Closing down the diaphragm (stopping down) generally increases resolution off-axis (away from the center) and enlarges the circle of good definition, both of which reach a maximum at a middle aperture, often f/22. Lens manufacturers measure and state in their literature the maximum coverage (or largest circle of good definition). Occasionally they will also list the minimum coverage, at full aperture.

Lens Design and Coverage

The working aperture is not the only factor affecting the size of the usable image circle (or covering circle). Some lenses are designed to have large covering circles while other lenses that may look similar are not. It is common to define the intrinsic coverage of a lens (a measure unaffected by the way the lens is used) by an angular measurement

The circle of coverage that is useful for photographing is the inner circle, slightly smaller than the entire projected circle of illumination. The image in the outer fringes of the circle of illumination can never be brought into good focus.

called a *field angle*. The field angle defines the shape of the cone of light projected from the rear of a lens that forms the covering circle at the film plane. Lens designers refer to the field angle as the *full-field angle* because they also use in their measurements the angle measured from the optical axis, called the *half-field angle*. You will probably see only the full-field angle quoted in any lens manufacturer's literature.

Few lenses used for view cameras have a field angle less than 55°, and the most common have field angles of 70°. The widest field angles for off-the-shelf lenses are just over 100°. Using a normal focal-length lens with a 70° field angle will give you a covering circle adequate for all but the most extreme movements. Chapter 7 tells how field angle is related to lens design, and what coverage to expect from most of the available lenses.

Below: Use this chart of coverage, field angle, and focal length to determine one of these values from the other two.

Peat, Isle of Skye, Scotland, 1972. *Emmet Gowin mounted a lens for a smaller camera on his 8x10 to make a series of photographs using the entire projected image circle. He has written that the use "of such a lens contributed to a particular description of space and that the circle itself was already a powerful form. Accepting the entire circle . . . involved a recognition of the inherent nature of things."*

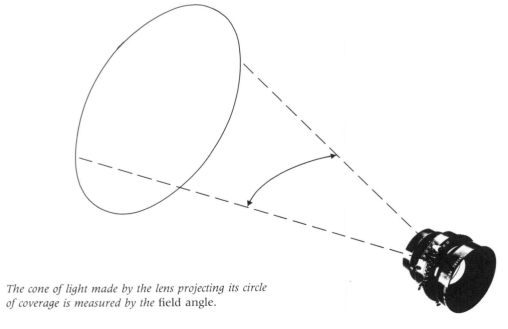

The cone of light made by the lens projecting its circle of coverage is measured by the field angle.

When a point in front of the camera is in focus, the distance from it to the lens is the object distance, and the distance from the lens to the film is the image distance.

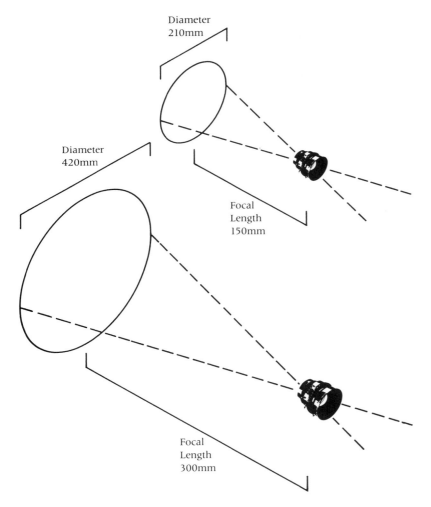

Diameter
210mm

Diameter
420mm

Focal
Length
150mm

Focal
Length
300mm

Of two lenses with the same field angle, the one with a greater focal length will have greater coverage. Doubling the focal length produces a covering circle with twice the diameter.

Focal Length and Coverage

When a point in front of the camera is in focus, the distance from it to the lens is called the *object distance*; the distance from the lens to the film is the *image distance*. For any object distance, there is a corresponding image distance. Focusing the camera means you are selecting an object distance by changing the image distance — by moving the film closer to or farther from the lens. As the object distance increases the image distance decreases, and vice versa. The shortest possible image distance corresponds to an object at infinity; for any lens this minimum image distance is called its *focal length*. Strictly speaking, the image distance is measured from the *rear nodal point* of the lens to the film (the rear nodal point is the point in the lens from which all the light seems to emanate; see Chapter 7). We cannot locate exactly the rear nodal point without specialized optical equipment, but for our purposes we may use the rear of the lensboard as a close enough approximation of its position.

The focal length of your lens directly affects the size of the image circle. For lenses of the same design, regardless of focal length, the field angle is the same. Therefore, the shape of the projected cone of light is the same. The size of the covering circle, however, is not the same. The longer of two lenses having the same field angle and focused at the same distance will cover a larger area because the film plane slices the cone of light farther from the lens. For example, a 150mm Nikkor-W has exactly the same field angle as a 300mm Nikkor-W: 70° at f/22. Measured also at f/22, the diameter of the image circle for the 150mm lens is 210mm, while for the 300mm lens it is 420mm. In this example, twice the focal length, with the same field angle, gives a covering circle twice the diameter.

Along with object distance, focal length determines the size the image will be on the negative. A longer lens makes a larger image for the same reason it projects a larger covering circle. Slicing the projected cone of light with the film at a greater distance makes every part of the image larger (for example, imagine moving a slide projector farther from its screen). For any object distance, a longer lens has a proportionately longer image distance than a shorter lens.

Image Distance and Coverage

Shortening the object distance also has the effect of enlarging the covering circle by increasing the image distance. For any lens, one focal length is its shortest usable image distance, corresponding to the greatest possible (infinity) object distance. As the object distance decreases from infinity, the image distance increases. In other words, as the object you are focusing on moves toward the camera, the distance between lens and film must increase for the object to remain in focus. An increase in image distance increases coverage in the same way that an increase in focal length does; a circle sliced from the projected cone of light gets larger as the distance of the slice from the lens increases. Focused at infinity, your lens has its least coverage.

Magnification ratio is the ratio of the size of the image to the size of the object. A magnification ratio of 1 occurs when image distance and object distance are equal — the image is the same size as the object. This is also sometimes called a 1:1 reproduction ratio. At 1:1, the image distance and object distance are equal and each is two times the focal length, using any lens. The covering circle then is twice its normal diameter. This enlarged covering circle means that for reproduction ratios around 1:1, you can use a lens with half the field angle or half the focal length you would need to use for distance. For closer work — for magnification greater than one — you can use even shorter lenses. For example, a lens with insufficient coverage for landscape use on 4x5 could be a satisfactory close-up lens for 8x10.

Angle of View

Angle of view determines how much of your subject is included in a photograph. Like the field angle, the angle of view is also an angular measurement of a cone, but the cone in front of the lens. Angle of view is a result of both focal length and film size; if you use the same focal-length lens to photograph the same scene from the same place on two different-sized pieces of film, the smaller film will record a smaller piece of the image, and consequently a smaller piece of the world. The smaller film produces a smaller angle of view. If instead you use two different focal-length lenses to photograph from the same place on two pieces of film the same size, the

To make these three photographs, a lens from a 120 roll-film camera was mounted on an 8x10. The first photograph was taken from a distance of several meters, and the size of the image circle is essentially that of infinity focus. The second photograph, from an object distance of less than a meter, shows slightly increased coverage from the increased image distance. The third, from an object distance about twice the 80mm focal length of the lens, required a much longer image distance. The greater the image distance, the farther the film is from the lens when it slices the projected cone of light, and the larger the covering circle.

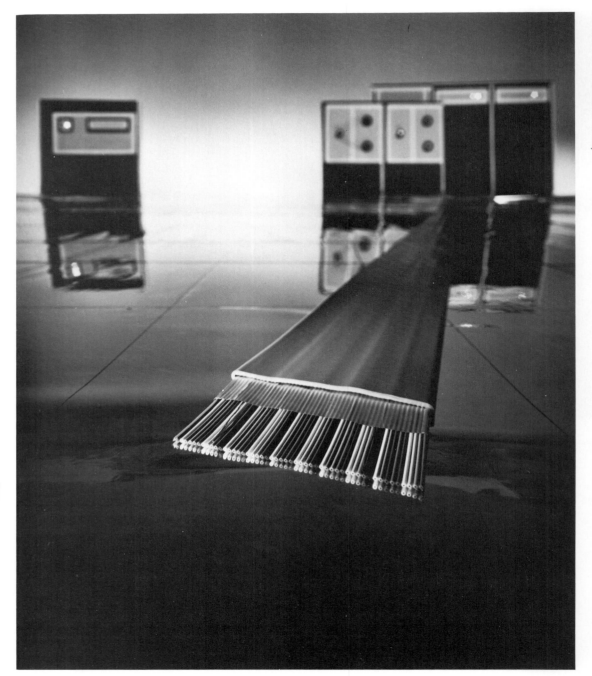

The object distance was so short, less than 100mm, that photographer Steve Grohe could use a 65mm lens designed for 4x5 to make this photograph on 8x10 (originally in color) and still have a covering circle larger than the film.

longer lens will record a smaller piece of the world because the image projected on the film is larger. The longer lens produces a smaller angle of view.

For any lens/film-size combination, the angle of view equals the smallest usable field angle for that focal-length lens — this field angle projects a circle with a diameter equal to the film diagonal. To just cover 4x5 film, for example, a 90mm lens needs a field angle of 81.5°, a 180mm lens needs a field angle of 46.6°. These angles tell you how much of the world each lens sees from any camera position. Notice that these two angles are *not* related by a factor of two, even though the focal lengths are. The diameter of the covering circle is proportional to the *sine* (a trigonometric ratio) of the field angle. The angle of view also gives you a clue to how much extra coverage (to accommodate movements) you

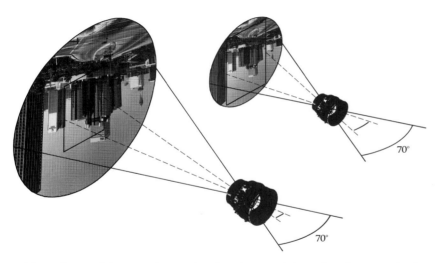

With two lenses of the same design (therefore the same field angle), the longer focal length projects the same image into a larger circle. With a piece of film the same size behind each lens, the one behind the longer lens will have an image of a smaller piece of the world. A longer lens, therefore, has a smaller angle of view than a shorter one in any given format.

With two lenses of different designs but the same focal length, the one with a wider field angle projects more of the same size image. Using the same size film with each will result in exactly the same picture. For any given film size, all lenses of the same focal length (as long as they cover the film) have the same angle of view.

have with the lens you are using, for example, if you had a 90mm lens with a field angle of 100°, or a 70° 180mm lens. The table on p. 77 shows the relationship between field angle or angle of view and covering circle or film size.

A 90mm lens on 4x5 film has the same angle of view as a 180mm lens on 8x10, the longer lens making an image twice as large on film having twice the dimensions. Having

the same angle of view, these focal-length/film-size combinations make images that appear the same, and both lenses need the same field angle to cover their respective films.

Comparisons of angle of view are difficult to make between formats with different *aspect ratios*, or frame shapes. If you try to find the lens for a 35mm camera that has the equivalent angle of view of a 180mm lens on 4x5, you will get too many correct answers because the 4x5 frame is a different shape from that of the 35mm. The angles of view across the short dimensions of each rectangle will be equal if you use a 45mm lens on the small camera. The long dimensions will have the same angle of view if you use a 55mm lens, and the diagonals have the same angle of view with a 50mm lens.

How Lenses Influence Perspective

Perspective, as we have found, refers to the relative sizes of objects and depends upon vantage point. Because of the difficulty of exactly translating three dimensions to two, the perspective in a photograph will be exactly the same as the eye would see from the lens position *only* if the angle of view of the lens is exactly the same as the angle of view of the eye viewing the photograph.

The angle of view of the eye viewing a photograph depends on the size of the print and its distance from the eye. So for a given print, the eye's angle of view will match that of the taking lens at only one viewing distance. To reproduce the exact perspective of a scene, then, a contact print — exactly the size of the negative — must be viewed from a distance the same as the lens was from the film when the picture was taken: the image distance. Enlarging the negative will have the same effect on correct viewing distance as using a longer focal-length lens; viewing distance for exact perspective will increase in proportion to the degree of enlargement.

It may not seem necessary to think about reproducing perspective so exactly in your photographs, but you should be aware of the interrelationship of focal length, film size, degree of enlargement, and viewing distance and of their effects on the appearance of perspective in your photographs. Most viewers of a photograph will automatically (and unconsciously) adjust their viewing distance to the size of the print, moving farther away

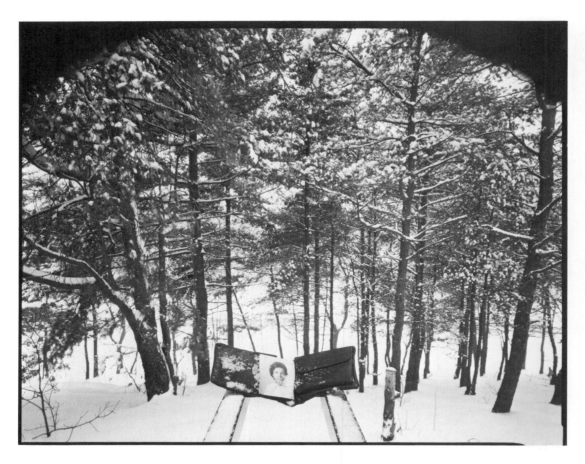

from a larger one and closer to a smaller one.
Most viewers find a comfortable distance to
be approximately the same as the diagonal of
the print. From this viewing distance, the exact perspective will be assured by making the
photograph with a lens having a focal length
equal to the film's diagonal. That is why this
focal length is referred to as *normal* for its
format. It is important to understand that any
photograph will reproduce exact perspective
from some viewing distance, but that distance may not be a comfortable one for the
viewer. Photographs made with wide-angle
(short focal-length) lenses are nearly always
viewed from too far away for exact perspective, which is why it is often assumed
(wrongly) that they distort it.

The Normal Lens

A normal lens for 4x5 film is 150mm (the
film's frame diagonal is actually 155mm),
normal for 5x7 is 210mm (actually 208mm),

and for 8x10 it is 300mm (actually 311mm). A normal design lens (see Chapter 7) with a field angle of about 70°, in the normal focal length for a given format, will offer enough extra coverage for moderate camera movements. Using a longer-than-normal focal length will make the image larger, the angle of view smaller, and the covering circle larger. For general use, many studio photographers use a 180mm (or longer) lens on 4x5 instead of a normal (150mm) because the increased coverage is useful for extreme movements, and the slight change to perspective from the necessarily longer object distance is not noticeable. A lens of longer-than-normal focal length is referred to as a *long-focus* lens; *telephoto* (a name many photographers mistakenly apply to all long-focus lenses) refers to a specific lens design (see p. 113), rarely used on view cameras.

The Wide-Angle Lens

A *wide-angle* is a lens of shorter-than-normal focal length for the format in use. As the focal length decreases, the field angle must increase to cover a given format. *Wide-field* lenses are those with field angles greater than normal. So a wide-angle lens must also be wide-field. A 165mm wide-field lens makes a good choice for a wide-angle lens for 8x10. The term wide-angle refers to an angle of view, while wide-field refers to a field angle. Although a wide-angle lens must be wide-field, the reverse is not true. On a 4x5 camera, a 165mm Super-Angulon, wide-field because of its 100° coverage, is not a wide-angle. Its focal length makes it a little longer than normal for 4x5. At one time, a lens with a field angle of 70° was considered a wide-field lens. That is now considered good performance for a normal lens, and a wide-field covers at least 90°.

Shutters

Two major types of shutter are used in to-day's cameras: the *leaf* shutter and the *focal-plane* (or curtain) shutter. Most small cameras have focal-plane shutters; the leaf shutter predominates in large-format photography.

The Focal-Plane Shutter

The focal-plane shutter is now designed into every 35mm single-lens-reflex (SLR) camera and many medium-format (120 film) cameras. In a 35mm camera, two curtains just in front of the film plane (sometimes called the focal plane) move across the film; one opens, beginning the exposure, and the other closes, ending it. This same shutter was once found in large-format use. The single-lens-reflex Graflex (p. 110), for example, was outfitted with a long spring-tensioned opaque cloth curtain with several horizontal openings, or slits, of varying widths. Positioned directly in front of the film, the curtain was drawn across the focal plane vertically between rollers for each exposure, and the shutter speed was determined by a combination of slit width and spring tension. The Speed Graphic press camera (see p. 105) was also equipped with a focal-plane shutter. Because these shutters had a top speed of 1/1000 of a second, they were especially desirable in a camera designed to be used hand-held, as were the Graphic and Graflex. The focal-plane shutter disappeared from large-format use as smaller cameras took over all hand-held photography in the 1950s. The position and size of a focal-plane shutter prevents its practical use on most of today's view cameras; its presence would impede the movements of the back.

The Leaf Shutter

The leaf shutter swings its closed blades, or leaves, outward on pivots until the entire light path of the lens is exposed. After a measured, timed exposure, it then swings them back to their original closed position. Because the blades are small and light, this action is much less likely to jar the camera during exposure than would the motion of a large focal-plane shutter. This sequence of blade movements, accelerating away from the cen-

Most view camera lenses use a leaf shutter, *which opens and closes by swinging a set of blades out of the light path and back. The leaves of this shutter are in their closed position.*

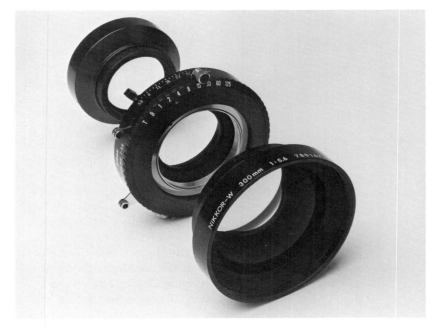

View camera lenses are shipped from the manufacturer already mounted in a be-tween-the-lens shutter. The front and rear halves of the lens can be unscrewed and removed from the shutter mount.

ter, stopping, and reversing direction to return, is not well suited to extremely fast shutter speeds; most leaf shutters are limited to a top speed of 1/500 of a second. Larger leaf shutters, such as those found on 8x10 camera lenses, have such large blades that 1/125 of a second is a common top speed. Fortunately, the use of high shutter speeds is extremely uncommon in large-format work.

Most view camera lenses are purchased already mounted *in shutter*, which means that the lens barrel is separated into two pieces and attached to the front and rear of a *between-the-lens* leaf shutter assembly, which is then mounted as one piece on the lensboard (p. 157). Each lens, then, must have its own shutter. As implied by its name, the between-the-lens shutter is mounted in an air space between the lens elements (see p. 113). The blades, usually five of them in a good shutter, can be seen through the front of the lens when the shutter is closed.

Between-the-lens leaf shutters are most often of the *preset*, or set-and-release, type. Moving one lever winds, or tensions, the spring that provides energy for the movement of the blades. Another lever, usually operated by a *cable release* (see p. 138), triggers the opening and closing of the blades for exposure. An *automatic*, or *press*, shutter has one lever that both winds and releases in one motion. Automatic shutters are limited in their range of fast speeds because the effort required to tension a shutter spring for a high speed would introduce camera movement. These shutters are useful on copy stand cameras (see p. 108) and any time a large number of exposures must be made with few adjustments.

Retarding Mechanism

Your shutter has a mechanism that opens the blades to reveal the entire light path and closes them to halt the exposure. A good shutter will complete these movements as rapidly as possible. In between opening and closing, the blades must stay out of the way for a measured, adjustable, and exactly repeatable amount of time — the exposure. Ensuring this precise delay is the job of the *retarding mechanism*.

In the early days of photography, when the shutter was only a lens cap, the only available retarding mechanism was the photographer's pocketwatch. Removing the lens cap began the exposure; covering the lens again ended it. The materials of early nineteenth-century photography in its infancy demanded exposures in sunlight measured in minutes, and it was not until more sensitive gelatin dry plates began to appear in the 1870s that this system finally succumbed to progress. Slightly less primitive shutter designs using gravity or rubber-band power had already been introduced, and tensioned-blade designs reaching 1/100 of a second (a presage of today's leaf shutters) were introduced in the 1880s.

By the turn of the century, the most satisfactory retarding mechanism was a pneumatic delay, which used a piston to force air through a small hole at the end of a cylinder. Substituting a smaller hole resulted in a longer delay, hence a slower shutter speed. Pneumatic-delay shutters were subject to timing variation from changes in temperature and humidity, and were easily immobilized by dust.

The introduction of the Ilex shutter in 1910 rapidly made all other designs obsolete. Its retarding mechanism, based upon the geared escapement of a mechanical watch,

The earliest shutter was a lens cap, and exposures were timed by pocketwatch. To assure a motionless portrait in those days, the sitter's head was held in a clamp.

provided accurate timing unaffected by humidity and all but the most extreme temperatures. Today's Copal shutter from Japan and the German Compur are direct descendants of the Ilex. Recently, shutters with electronic delay mechanisms have become available; their speed settings are extremely accurate and their timing invariant. These new shutters are still considerably more expensive than those with mechanical delays, however, and the difference in accuracy is inconsequential to most working photographers.

Shutter Speeds

Your shutter is marked with a series of *shutter speeds* and calibrated so that each speed corresponds to an exposure time, or the duration that the shutter is open. The markings indicate the denominator in a fraction of a second. For example, 30 marked on the shutter dial stands for 1/30 of a second exposure. Today's shutters, by convention, all have a sequence of speeds like this:

1	2	4	8	15	30	60
	125	250	500			

This sequence was adopted in the 1950s to conform closely to the exact one-stop interval used for the aperture sequence. Many shutters from before that time, some of which are still in use, had a slightly more irregular scale:

1	2	5	10	25	50
	100	200	400		

Exposures longer than one second are accommodated by one of two additional settings, T and B. Some shutters provide only the B, which stands for *bulb*. This setting will hold the shutter open as long as the release lever is pressed or the cable release is held. The name refers to early shutters, which were operated by air pressure supplied by a rubber bulb. The shutter opened when the bulb was squeezed, stayed open while it was held, and closed when it was released. The T setting, for *time*, opens the shutter with one stroke of the release lever, and closes it with another. Use this setting if your shutter has no press-focus lever to hold open the shutter for viewing.

The *press-focus* lever (or pre-view button) on your shutter allows you to open and close its blades manually without readjusting the speed selector. Because a view camera uses the same lens for viewing and focusing that it

The pneumatic-delay shutter, popular for the last decade of the nineteenth century, relied upon air being squeezed out of a small hole in a cylinder to regulate exposures.

uses to make the exposure, you need to be able to open and close its shutter easily. Use the press-focus to hold open the shutter for viewing and focusing. Some shutters must be tensioned before the press-focus will operate. Automatic shutters are made without press-focus levers and must be set on T (or B, using a locking cable release) for viewing.

Shutter Efficiency

The design of your leaf shutter's mechanism can produce an unexpected inaccuracy in your exposures as a result of variations in *shutter efficiency*. Shutter efficiency is a measure of the difference between the shutter speed you set, or the *indicated shutter speed*, and the actual time of exposure, the *effective shutter speed*. This difference is due to the time the shutter blades take to travel from a closed to a fully open position, and from open to closed. When you change from one shutter speed to another, you only alter the delay time during which the blades are held open. The blade travel time is additional, and with most shutters it is the same for all settings.

As the blades travel, opening like an iris diaphragm, the center of the light path opens before and closes after its outer edge. The shutter, therefore, fully reveals a very small

These are contemporary between-the-lens leaf shutters, with (a) shutter-speed dial (b) aperture dial and indicator (c) press-focus lever (d) cable release attachment point and release lever (e) pc synchronization connector, and (f) wind lever.

aperture in a shorter time than it does a wide aperture. With the smallest apertures, the entire light path is open for almost the entire duration of the exposure. With wider apertures the blades must travel farther after their release to uncover the entire light path, and they begin to cover it sooner on their return. At any setting, the shutter is therefore giving full exposure for less time at larger apertures than at smaller ones. As you increase the aperture, the effective shutter speed will lag farther behind the indicated shutter speed. This discrepancy means the shutter is less efficient for larger apertures.

If you select a slow shutter speed, the blade travel time is a very small part of the overall exposure, and the difference in shutter efficiency between large and small apertures is insignificant. With the faster shutter speeds, however, the blades barely reach their fully open position before they begin to close, and they are moving during most of the exposure. At faster speeds, then, the difference in shutter efficiency between large and small apertures noticeably increases.

Manufacturers normally calibrate their shutters to be accurate (100% efficient) at their widest aperture by adjusting the delay time between the half-open and half-closed positions to equal the indicated shutter speed. The efficiency difference, then, will give your film more exposure than you expect at the smaller apertures rather than less than you expect at larger apertures. The effects of changing shutter efficiency will probably be noticeable only at faster shutter speeds. In practice, small apertures are seldom combined with fast shutter speeds, but the compounded error can result in as much as a full stop of overexposure. In addition, since shutters are more prone to slow down than to speed up with age, mechanical error often compounds the problem by increasing the overexposure error.

Self-Timer

Although unusual in current leaf shutters, many view camera shutters made in the last few decades (and still in use) included a *self-timer*. After the shutter's release is pressed, a self-timer provides a delay of several seconds before the blades move, to allow the photographer to get into the picture or just away from the camera. The self-timer was often incorporated into the wind mechanism; by moving a latch, the winding lever could be moved beyond its normal end position to wind the self-timer. Available today is an accessory self-timer with a cable-release tip and a selector for several delay times. Remote-control releases operated by radio are also available.

Shutter Synchronization

When you use an electronic flash, commonly called *strobe*, or the all-but-obsolete flashbulbs, the job of *synchronization* falls to the shutter. Because the flash is a short-duration light, an automatic mechanical or electronic switch must be used to trigger the illumination so it appears when the shutter is open: that is, to synchronize the flash with the shutter.

Before the popularity of strobe light for the professional photographer eliminated the common use of flashbulbs, synchronization made shutter design and use very complex. Flashbulbs were manufactured in several sizes, and required different shutter delays for proper synchronization. Bulbs, once ignited, take as much as 1/30 of a second to reach maximum brightness, and another 1/30 of a second to die out. In order to efficiently use a shutter speed shorter than 1/15 of a second, a delay system similar to a shutter's retarding mechanism was needed to open the shutter at a specific time after igniting the bulb. Properly adjusted, this synchronization would open the shutter at the time of maximum light output.

Early synchronizers for flashbulbs often were shutter accessories consisting of a separate delay piston attached to the shutter or lensboard, which offered three delay settings for three classes of bulbs: F (.005 seconds), M (.014–.020 seconds), and S (.030 seconds). As electronic flash began to appear in the early 1940s, shutters were made with internal synchronization to accommodate it. Because electronic flash reaches its peak light output almost instantaneously, proper synchronization needs only to trigger the flash when the shutter is fully open. A simple electrical contact inside the shutter is all that is needed, making the shutter less expensive than one with synchronization for bulbs. Also, without the necessity of a timed delay, synchronization is more dependable. The designation X is used to indicate triggering at the instant the full-open position is reached. Shutters made today offer only X-synchronization.

Many shutters were made between the introduction of strobe light and the obsolescence of bulbs and have both internal M- and X-synchronization. These shutters have a small selector switch. If you have a shutter with such a switch, and you use only strobes, tape the switch in the X position to avoid a possible catastrophe. If you inadvertently use the M position, the light from your strobe will have disappeared by the time the shutter opens, and your exposure will be considerably less than you expect. If you have a modern shutter with only X-synchronization, you can still use flashbulbs by selecting a shutter speed of 1/30 or longer so the shutter remains open long enough to capture all the illumination.

Shortly after its introduction, electronic flash earned the nickname "speedlight" from its extremely short duration; flash times shorter than 1/2000 of a second were common. Strobes were used to stop action, and could be synchronized with a leaf shutter at its top speed. As electronic flash for the studio evolved, power supplies were made safer and less expensive by using lower internal voltage. The use of lower operating voltage has created a side effect, however. It lengthens the duration of the flash, and many studio flash units must now be used with X-synchronization at shutter speeds no faster than 1/125 of a second.

Synch Connectors
Synchronization depends on an electronic signal transmitted from the shutter to the

This remarkable series of photographs was made by Dr. Harold Edgerton of a mechanical shutter opening and closing at a shutter speed of 1/200 second. Thirty-nine pictures were taken in that time at a rate of 4200 per second using a high-speed strobe. These photographs show the problem of shutter efficiency; the shutter was completely open for less than one-fourth of the exposure time.

Stopping the flight of this bullet traveling at 900 meters per second required very accurate synchronization with a 1/300,000 second flash. Dr. Harold Edgerton made this photograph at the Massachusetts Institute of Technology in 1964.

flash to trigger the light at the correct time. Although invisible infrared transmitters and receivers are turning up in high-rent studios, your signal for synchronization is likely to be transmitted from shutter to flash unit by a wire called a *synch cable*. This wire has a connector at each end — one to plug into a receptacle on the outside of the shutter body, and one to join with the strobe. The connectors on your cable must mate properly with those on your shutters and flash. In universal use now is the *PC connector*, and all currently manufactured between-the-lens shutters have a PC receptacle. An older shutter may have a *standard*, or two-pin plug, for which adapters are available. Most studio strobe power packs accept a standard AC lampcord plug, and any household extension cord may be used as a synch extension. You will still need a short PC cord to connect the extension to your shutter.

The Diaphragm

Your between-the-lens shutter also houses a *diaphragm*, the mechanism that adjusts the light intensity admitted to the film. It is sometimes called an *iris* diaphragm because its function corresponds to the iris of the human eye. With blades similar to those of the shutter, the diaphragm creates a circular opening centered in the light path — the aperture. The aperture is measured by f/numbers, each a ratio of the diaphragm opening diameter to the lens focal length.

The diaphragm's blades pivot and slide over one another to change the size of the aperture. These blades are visible through the rear element of the lens or, when the shutter is open, through the front. They should retract entirely out of view when set to the maximum aperture.

Since there is no distinct advantage to a perfectly circular diaphragm, most have as few as five blades to fit the narrow air space in modern design lenses. The aperture will appear to be a rounded polygon. The aperture settings, or f/stops, are usually indicated on the front and side of the shutter dial on the *aperture ring*. A pointer or mark on the dial may be moved to set and indicate your working aperture. Sometimes the settings and pointer appear twice — 180° apart — so they can be seen from above and below, or from the right and left.

Some aperture rings are provided with detent (or click-stop) settings at whole-stop intervals, some have detents at $\frac{1}{2}$ or $\frac{1}{3}$ stop intervals, and others slide smoothly across their entire range. In all cases, however, the pointer or mark indicates the exact aperture, and settings in between whole stops provide for smaller increments of exposure. With the shutter speeds, on the other hand, selecting a position between two adjacent settings (for example, between 1/30 and 1/60) will cause the shutter to choose one or the other, but will not produce an intermediate shutter speed and may damage the shutter.

The position of the diaphragm along the optical axis is an important aspect of lens design because it controls *focus shift*. A lens with a focus shift changes the image distance with aperture, so if you focus once with the aperture at its maximum and then close down to a smaller working aperture, you must refocus after stopping down. Once refocused, the optical performance of a lens with focus shift is otherwise unaffected by it. Some view-

The diaphragm is the multibladed mechanism that creates and adjusts the aperture.

Before adjustable diaphragms became common, apertures were selected and changed with the use of Waterhouse Stops. *Each stop was an individual flat paddle with the appropriately sized opening, and was inserted into a slot in the lens barrel for use.*

camera lenses, notably nineteenth-century designs, exhibit focus shift because the designer could not place the diaphragm in the optimum position, usually because there was already an element there. Today's computer-designed lenses are mostly without focus shift problems.

Behind-the-Lens Shutters

If you use several lenses with the same camera, it may be to your advantage to have one *behind-the-lens* shutter. This separate shutter is not a part of a lens as are the between-the-lens types; it mounts to the camera and can then be used with all your lenses. With it, you can use lenses mounted *in barrel*, that is, without a shutter. Like a small-format lens, barrel-mounted lenses have all the glass parts (elements) of the lens enclosed in a single tube rather than separated into two pieces to be mounted in the front and back of a shutter. As a result, you don't buy a shutter with each lens, and the lenses are less expensive.

A behind-the-lens shutter will give you exactly the same shutter speeds for each lens. If your work demands exact calibration of shutter speeds — necessary for the Zone System — the speed variation between shutters when each lens has its own can add enormously to already ponderous calculations. This is not to say that the accuracy of behind-the-lens shutter speeds is any better — they are subject to the inaccuracies of any mechanical shutter — but the inaccuracies are more predictable since you are always using the same shutter.

The studio photographer who controls exposure with aperture and strobe brightness uses a shutter only to synchronize the flash and to open the lens to focus. Any shutter will suffice for these basic applications, but the Sinar behind-the-lens shutter allows you to adjust the aperture from behind the camera, and couples with the spring back to close the shutter when the film holder is inserted. These features save time and streamline camera operation, particularly when a studio setup requires that lights, stands, reflectors, or shades be next to the lens. Such a setup often obstructs access to the shutter's controls.

The behind-the-lens shutter does have some limitations. Its mounting position prevents its use with some wide-angle lenses. These lenses have such a limited back-focus distance that there is inadequate space to fit the shutter between the rear of the lens and the ground glass. Another disadvantage of the mounting position is that the light path through the shutter is wider than through a conventional between-the-lens position and necessitates larger shutter blades. The increased inertia of heavier blades lowers the possible top speed and aggravates the exposure errors resulting from variations in shutter efficiency. And even though barrel-mounted lenses are less expensive than those in shutters, don't expect an overall savings — a good behind-the-lens shutter can cost as much as six of the between-the-lens shutters it replaces.

Although it is an anachronism, the venerable Packard shutter is still available. A throwback to the mid-nineteenth century, this bulb-only behind-the-lens shutter is still surprisingly useful. Simple and inexpensive, the Packard shutter allows you to use older barrel-mount lenses that are usually a fraction of the cost of new lenses. The Packard restricts you to the use of two shutter speeds: B for a second or longer, and approximately 1/25 of a second. Long exposures are very common with large-format photography, and the Packard at a second or more is every bit as accurate as any other shutter. If you use strobes, a professional repair shop can adapt an X-synch connection to the 1/25 speed to give you a simple, inexpensive shutter suitable for most studio uses.

This sophisticated behind-the-lens shutter allows you to adjust the shutter speed and aperture and to open and close the lens without leaving your viewing position behind the camera.

The anachronistic Packard shutter is inexpensive, practical, and dependable, and may save you money when you buy lenses.

6 Cameras

The camera obscura predated the invention of photography by centuries. It projected an image that could be traced, and was used as an artist's aid for naturalistic drawing.

The cameras Alphonse Giroux made for his brother-in-law L. J. M. Daguerre were the world's first production cameras. This is a photograph of an exact working replica.

All cameras are descendants of the *camera obscura*, an optical curiosity predating the Renaissance adopted by artists to aid in realistic drawing. As its Latin name ("dark chamber") suggests, it is essentially a box or room with a pinhole or lens in one wall to form an image on the opposite wall.

The Development of the View Camera

The earliest photographic cameras on record were made by or for the inventors of photography. Joseph Nicèphore Nièpce of France and England's William Henry Fox Talbot, two men with reasonable (but not exclusive) claim to be photography's inventor, used simple wooden boxes. These boxes evolved gradually into today's view camera. It occurred to Talbot in 1839 to cut holes in the camera's back to enable him to see if the paper calotype negative was in focus. In the same year, L. J. M. Daguerre, a Frenchman who invented the Daguerreotype and claimed himself to be the inventor of photography, designed the first camera to be commercially produced. Made by Alphonse Giroux in Paris, it was also a wooden box, but was assembled from two nesting boxes made to slide in and out of one another for focusing, and it featured a focusing screen at the back.

The Flatbed

In 1851, an American camera introduced the bellows to common use, and became recognizable as an early view camera. As a result of the bellows, the early 1850s gave rise to a number of folding camera designs. The use of a flexible bellows required cameras to have a baseboard to support the camera, and until the monorail began to gain popularity in the 1940s, virtually all view cameras were a variation on the *flatbed* camera.

The enlarger appeared in the 1860s, but its practicality was severely limited by the slow speed of the available printing materials until the beginning of the twentieth century. Without enlarging, photographs can only be made the same size as the negative, so to the

William Henry Jackson was one of several photographers who documented the topography of the American West in the latter nineteenth century as the land was being tamed by settlement. He used flatbed view cameras and glass-plate negatives as large as 20x24 inches in rugged terrain.

The desire for ever larger photographs gave rise to some absurdities in the days before enlarging. This camera was evidently assembled for only one use — to photograph a steam train onto plates 4½x8 feet.

This half-plate Daguerreotype camera, made around 1850 by H. J. Lewis in New York, displayed the first use of a bellows in a camera body.

early photographers, making large photographs meant using a large camera. To produce photographs in a scale appropriate to the grandeur of the American West, William Henry Jackson, Carleton Watkins, Timothy O'Sullivan, and others spent the 1860s, '70s, and '80s climbing pinnacles and fording streams with cameras large enough to produce 20x24-inch negatives. If a camera the size of a steamer trunk seems enough of a burden, remember that negatives in those days were made on glass plates, so the pack animals (and photographers) were also saddled with bundles of heavy, fragile glass.

By the 1880s flatbed cameras had evolved into what remained the standard professional's tool for the next seventy years. The most common form of flatbed camera had a base made of a double wooden supporting track with metal gears for focusing, and used track extensions to extend the bellows for long focal-length lenses. Although many are still in use, no cameras of this type are made today. A good used flatbed camera can be an economical way to begin working in large format.

By the end of the nineteenth century, three different designs for flatbed cameras were in common use. Most popular was the *tailboard* camera, with a front standard fixed to the front of the baseboard and a focusing track behind it. The fixed lens position made close-up work easier, and the design eliminated obstructions to the field of view in front of the lens. Folding versions were made for portability; the track folded up on hinges just behind the rear standard. William Henry Jackson used a very large tailboard camera to make his mammoth landscape photographs in the latter half of the 1870s.

The second flatbed style, for which there is no generic name, had a focusing track, often hinged, fixed to the back of the camera and extending forward. The front standard was made to slide along this track for focusing. Often the bellows were tapered, to collapse into a smaller space than did those with parallel sides. The only flatbed cameras currently produced — technical, press, and field cameras — evolved from this design.

More versatile than either of the other early flatbed designs and appearing in the 1870s were models featuring movable front and rear standards, and front and rear base rails that folded up from a fixed center section.

Mahogany was the favored material for camera bodies, and time has proven it a wise selection. Given reasonable care, most wooden cameras have lasted in nearly original condition. Special versions of standard

This 11x14 Sky Scraper camera made by Folmer and Schwing at the time of their merger with Eastman Kodak in 1905 is a classic example of the flatbed view camera. The back swings and tilts, with no lateral movements, and the front has a vertical shift. The body parts are mahogany and brass.

This German Leubel camera from around 1880 is a version of a flatbed view. Because the front is fixed on the focusing track and only the back moves, it is called a tailboard *camera.*

Teak was used in this tropical camera for its resistance to the effects of hot, humid climates.

Certainly the progenitor of the modern monorail view, Joseph Petzval's 1857 camera had a double-extension bellows and a triangular wooden rail.

The first all-metal view camera, this Graphic View 4x5 was produced from 1941 to 1948.

designs were made of teak, to withstand heat and humidity in tropical climates. Before the postwar popularity of monorails, metal construction was an occasional curiosity in large-format camera construction.

Monorail Cameras

The first monorail cameras were probably patterned after the *optical bench*, a straight rail used in optical research to hold elements in precise alignment. Although several designs appeared in the 1850s, no monorail of lasting popularity surfaced until nearly a century later. All-metal monorail designs originated in the United States with the Graphic View, introduced in 1941, and in Europe with the Swiss Sinar, first sold in 1948. Current models include Japan's Horseman, Toyo, and Wista, Cambo from Holland, Arca and Sinar from Switzerland, Germany's Linhof and Plaubel, India's Rajah, and the American Calumet.

Design and manufacturing differences create a wide range of prices, but the essential function of photographing is little different from one monorail camera to another. The basic differences show up in ease of use, availability of accessories, and sturdiness. The quality of your images will be entirely dependent upon the quality of your optics and your abilities as a photographer.

Descendants of the Flatbed Camera

Field Cameras

Like a harpsichord in an era of electric pianos, the *field camera* seems a charming anachronism. It is the last vestige of a long tradition of wooden cameras, and the beauty and warmth of the materials belie the down-to-earth practicality of this professional tool.

A field camera is a folding flatbed camera designed specifically for compactness and portability. The bed folds up into the back, creating its own storage compartment for the bellows and front. Most designs offer swing and tilt on both the front and the rear, as well as a rising and falling front. Almost unchanged from its turn-of-the-century design, the field camera is our closest link with the numerous folding flatbed cameras that were the mainstay of photography from the mid-nineteenth century until World War II.

The venerable Deardorff, the name almost synonymous with wooden field cameras, has been made in Chicago continually and virtually without change since 1923. Deardorff's 4x5 camera has a reversing back. The slightly larger 5x7, called a 5x7 Special, can be used as a revolving-back 4x5. Deardorff also makes an 8x10 and an occasional 11x14 in the same design as the 4x5. For years, the only field cameras available were the Deardorff and the similar Gandolfi, which was made in Britain until 1981. A recent surge of interest in folding cameras has caused the introduction of America's Calumet Wood-Field, and the import of wooden

The Deardorff cameras are the best-known field cameras and have been manufactured virtually unchanged since 1923.

The 8x10 Toyo is the only metal field camera available in that format. The 4x5 Calumet has the unusual option of a format-increasing 5x7 back.

The larger Toyo features interchangeable bellows, and the Calumet can be folded with a lens in place.

A simple, elegant solution to the problem of how to make a long, rectangular photograph was the Banquet camera — a long, rectangular camera.

One of the most curious solutions to the wide-photograph problem was this Goerz Hypergon wide-field lens. It attempted to correct off-axis light falloff with a center-weighted propeller mounted in front of the lens. A squeeze of the air bulb set the propeller in motion just before exposure.

Wista, Ikeda, Nagaoka, and Tachihara cameras from Japan and Rajah field views from India. Calumet's Wood-Field is a 4x5, with an optional 5x7 adapter back, and has the thoughtful feature of a hole in the bed large enough to allow the camera to be folded up with the lens in place. Wista makes a 4x5 and an 8x10 available in rosewood or cherry. Toyo, in Japan, makes a sturdy metal-bodied field camera in 4x5 and 8x10 formats. The Toyo Field 8x10 is the only field camera to accept interchangeable bellows.

If you need a camera with full movements, yet want one that is light and compact enough to pack and transport easily, a field camera is your best choice.

Banquet Cameras

In 1913, a curious offspring of the flatbed view camera appeared when Folmer and Schwing introduced their *Banquet* camera in Rochester, N.Y. This was a view camera of normal design which made abnormally shaped photographs. The long, horizontal image was not, however, without precedent.

From the time of Fox Talbot, the desire to depart from the classic proportions of the golden rectangle and the problem of how best to produce a wide panoramic photograph led photographers to seek some unusual solutions. Some photographers pieced together several photographs of ordinary shape, while others tried special cameras with rotating lenses, rotating cameras, curved glass plates, conical reflectors, and spherical, water-filled lenses.

The simple solution, it seemed, was an ordinary camera design, altered to take a flat sheet of ordinary film in a long, rectangular shape. This was the Banquet camera, made in 7x17 and 12x20-inch formats, and intended to use 13- and 16-inch wide-field lenses. The 5x12, 7x17, and 8x20 Korona Panoramic Views were introduced in 1926, the year Folmer and Schwing discontinued the Banquet. All the Banquet and Korona film sizes correspond to half (lengthwise) of one of the then-common standard sheet-film sizes. The photographer with an 8x20 Korona, for example, could cut down sheets of readily-available 16x20 film.

Although used Banquet and Korona cameras are frequently available from antique camera dealers, film holders are scarce and film cut to the correct sizes is available only by special order in large quantities.

E. O. Goldbeck's photograph of a human insignia was made at Kelly Air Force Base in San Antonio, Texas, in 1926 with an 8x20 Korona Panoramic View.

Allen Hess made Mrs. Evelyn, Lafitte, Louisiana *with the camera shown above. He attached a back from an 8x20 Korona to the accessory bracket of his Sinar Monorail to give him all the advantages of a modular banquet camera.*

Press Cameras

Until the middle of the 1950s the archetypal press photographer (now called a photojournalist) was clutching a Speed Graphic. Almost unchanged from its introduction in 1912 until production ceased in 1970, this ubiquitous press camera recorded celebrations and disasters, World Series and world wars. Once film emulsions became fine and fast enough to make quality enlargements from "miniature" (an early nickname for 35mm) negatives, the press corps shifted its allegiance en masse to the smaller format.

As a result, the once-proud workhorse of the front page is now in the classified ads. Versatile, durable, and inexpensive, the used press camera is undoubtedly the best value in photo equipment. At least one manufacturer still produces a Speed Graphic look-alike, but like the plush splendor of "Detroit Iron" cars

of the 1950s, the halcyon days of the press camera's popular appeal have passed.

Designed for portability, press cameras offer features useful for work outside the studio. The focusing track, on which the front standard rides, nests into a bed that folds on hinges into the rear of the camera body. When shut, the camera body itself forms a protective box — a built-in carrying case. A normal lens can be left in place with the front folded for quick setup. The ground-glass back has a hinged cover that often doubles as a focusing hood and helps further protect the closed camera against damage.

Because press cameras were used for a variety of assignments, they were often fitted with multiple viewing and focusing devices. It was not uncommon to augment the ground glass with a top-mounted viewfinder and a wire-frame sports finder, in addition to a focusing rangefinder.

Although by 1940 Graphic models included a front shift, movements on many press cameras are limited to those used most often: the front rise and the lens tilt. Most press cameras have a *drop bed*, the equivalent of a rear-standard bottom-axis tilt, to allow the use of a wide-angle lens without vignetting by the bed. But because the camera was most often hand-held, these movements were largely ignored.

The history of the press camera in America is the history of the Speed Graphic. It was introduced in 1912 by the Folmer and Schwing Company, which had been a division of Eastman Kodak since 1905. As part of an antitrust settlement, Kodak divested themselves of the company, by then called Century-Folmer, and it became Folmer Graflex in 1926, and Graflex, Inc. in 1945.

The first Speed Graphic was a compact, folding, large-format camera with a built-in focal-plane shutter to allow the use of barrel-mounted lenses. The mahogany bodies were made in four formats, from $3\frac{1}{4}x4\frac{1}{4}$ to 5x7, and were covered with leather. The camera was probably introduced as a compact, portable large-format camera, but a model change in 1928 anticipated its use as an action camera by moving the handle from the top to the side and adding a wire frame finder. The Pacemaker series of Graphic cameras in 1947 added coupled-rangefinder focusing and introduced the Crown Graphic, a version made lighter by the omission of the focal-plane shutter. Production of the Crown Graphic continued until 1973, when the company folded.

Technical Cameras

Along with the press and field cameras, the technical camera evolved from the fixed-back flatbed camera design. It incorporates the best features of its predecessors into a versatile machine for contemporary uses. As opposed to the press camera, which was built for the action photographer and, almost as an afterthought, could be used on a tripod, the modern technical camera was designed as a view camera with full movements with the option of being used hand-held.

Technical cameras all close in the same manner as press cameras: the bed folds into the back, forming a protective box. The spring back is connected to the body with four sliding pins, allowing each corner of the back to be positioned independently. This system gives the technical camera the back

The Crown Graphic, Speed Graphic's look-alike without the built-in focal-plane shutter, was made until 1973.

The Horseman Technical Camera has the features of a Linhof Technika but uses nothing larger than 120 and 220 roll film.

movements missing from otherwise similar press cameras.

The archetypal technical camera is the German Linhof Technika, which has been manufactured in Munich with constant improvements since 1936. Valentin Linhof began as a maker of shutters and by 1899 added cameras to his line. In 1910 Linhof began to make an all-metal folding camera that was the direct predecessor of the Technika. A burst of innovation produced the prototype Technika in 1936. It incorporated a fully adjustable swing back, which had been patented two years earlier. The Super Technika of 1946 introduced a built-in rangefinder with cams to couple it to interchangeable lenses of various focal lengths. The current Technika models, 6x7cm, 4x5, and 5x7, incorporate rear swing and tilt and a full-movement front with coupled-rangefinder focusing and an accurate viewfinder corrected for *parallax* error (parallax is the difference between what is seen by the lens and by the viewfinder due to the slight difference in their vantage points). Technika cameras are remarkable examples of engineering and manufacturing precision, and sell for almost as much as a new car.

A much less expensive 4x5 technical camera than the Technika is Wista's 45, the only similar large-format camera made today. It is made in versions with and without lens swing, interchangeable bellows, and coupled rangefinder. An optional 5x7 back is also available. The Calumet Horseman is a useful, smaller version of the technical camera, designed for 120 and 220 roll film only.

If you need a portable camera with full movements, more sturdiness than a field camera, and the option of hand-held use, you will want to shop for a technical camera.

This all-metal Linhof folding camera from 1924 was the forerunner of the Technika series of technical view cameras.

Linhof's Master Technika is fully adjustable, and includes coupled-rangefinder focusing and a parallax-corrected viewfinder.

This vertical process camera from Nu-Arc might be found in the office of a graphic artist.

Another version of the vertical process camera, Polaroid's MP-4, is known as a copy camera, *and is well suited to making slides and copy negatives from flat originals.*

Process Cameras

The needs of the graphic arts industry have generated a number of specialized camera designs based on the flatbed view camera, called *process* cameras. Sometimes called *copy*, *repro*, or *stat* cameras, vertical and horizontal process cameras are designed specifically to make reproductions near the original size of flat copy.

The printing industry uses process cameras to make *halftones* and *color separations*. Both are dot-patterned images on high-contrast litho film that are "burned," or exposed, directly onto the printing plate for an offset press. At least one of these dot-patterned negatives is necessary for every photograph reproduced in print, and there are probably more process cameras in use than all other view cameras combined. These cameras are often permanently installed in a room with the bellows, lens, copyboard, and lights separated by a wall from the back. The back is in a separate room, usually a processing darkroom. Focus is read from published charts of magnification and set by calibrated distance scales.

Nu-Arc's horizontal process camera seems distant from the nineteenth-century flatbeds, but the lineage is direct.

Paul Strand's photograph of Alfred Steiglitz from about 1929 shows him with his Graflex, with which he probably made his Equivalent series of cloud photographs.

A process camera is used only for its ability to photograph onto large sheets of film and is therefore designed to have no movements. The lens and film planes are fixed in a parallel position. The camera's back, hinged on the side for film loading, swings out to accept a sheet of film directly on its front surface. No film holders are used. Drawing a vacuum through an array of tiny holes on the back's surface holds the film motionless and flat during exposure.

A small, freestanding, vertical process camera for a designer's office or typesetting shop might accommodate film up to 14x17, while a larger, built-in horizontal model for a production printer can use film as large as 60 inches square.

Lenses specially designed for process work (*apochromats*, p. 126) are optimized by the lens designer for the most common reproduction ratios, and carefully corrected against aberrations for the printer's specific primary colors. Process lenses are made in an array of very long focal lengths (commonly up to 1800mm and sometimes longer), to cover the large sheets of film common in the industry. These lenses are almost always mounted in barrel, since the exposure in process cameras is controlled by switching the lights on and off.

Reflex Cameras

A *reflex* camera produces an image on a ground-glass surface parallel to the optical axis by placing a mirror at a 45° angle to the light path. This allows the film to be in place during viewing and focusing. Although the principle predates photography — it was introduced in the seventeenth-century camera obscura — the design emerged slowly. Today, however, (35mm) reflex cameras dominate the photography market.

The first camera with a reflex design was patented in 1861 by the English photographer Thomas Sutton. Sutton's camera had an internal mirror to reflect the lens image up to a horizontal ground glass set into the top of the camera. Before exposure, the mirror was swung on hinges from its viewing position into a position covering the opening for the ground glass, making the camera's interior lighttight. Sutton's camera was not popular, due in part to the wet-plate process then used. Because the plate needed to be sensitized immediately before use (and exposed

The Naturalist Graflex was a large-format single-lens-reflex Graflex with a 600mm lens. A similar camera called "Big Bertha" was a common sight with press photographers at sporting events. The standard Graflex shown here was the last model made: a Super D.

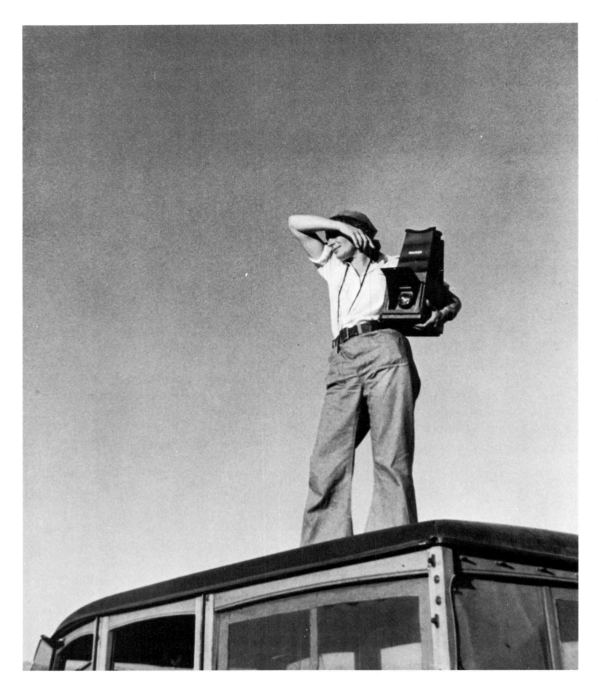

and developed while wet) there was little advantage to making it possible to view and focus rapidly. With the emergence of practical dry plates in the 1880s came a flood of hand cameras, and the reflex became a popular design.

In 1901, the Folmer and Schwing Company (which also made the Speed Graphic) introduced the Graflex, which became the most popular series of large-format single-lens-reflex cameras. First made in four sizes from 4x5 to 8x10, the Graflex family was

manufactured in several incarnations until it was finally discontinued in 1963. In the six decades of its production, the features of the Graflex were modernized slowly, but its basic design remained unchanged. It was similar to the Sutton camera, with a large internal reflex mirror, and was designed so that its top viewing hood (to darken the area around the ground glass), lens, and bellows would fold into the body, forming a protective, portable box in the shape of a cube. Versions of the basic camera included double-lens stereo cameras and "Big Bertha" Graflexes adapted to lenses with focal lengths as long as 40 inches. The Super D was the last Graflex model, and in 4x5 format remains a useful camera.

An unusual set of *twin-lens reflex* cameras is marketed currently by Peter Gowland in California. First made by Gowland in 1956 for his own use in photographing glamour models, the Gowlandflex is now made and sold in 4x5 and 5x7, with a wide-angle version available in 4x5. These cameras use matched lenses in pairs, one to form an image on a ground glass for viewing and the other to form an image on the film. With a twin-lens camera there need be no delay between final viewing and exposure because the presence of a film holder does not block the ground-glass screen. A cam on each camera corrects parallax error, which increases with decreasing object distance. A similar TLR 4x5 camera was made for a short time in Holland by Cambo.

The only large-format twin-lens-reflex camera made today is the Gowlandflex.

This odd-looking hybrid made by Arca is a single-lens-reflex monorail view camera.

The Cambo-Wide is a special-purpose 4x5 camera made to take only a 90mm wide-field lens.

7 More About Lenses

Although you needn't study optical engineering to be able to use a large-format camera, there are advantages to knowing the evolution of the modern lens and the constraints within which lens designers must work. This knowledge not only will enable you to be an enlightened consumer of used and new equipment but will also help you understand the optical limitations you will face each time you make a photograph.

The first part of this chapter will familiarize you with the general anatomy of a lens and with the challenges facing lens designers. As in any other complex field, the terminology of lens design is very specific. Some of the specific terms have other or broader meanings in casual conversation, but they are defined for their technical meanings here. The second half of this chapter traces the history of modern camera lenses, with emphasis on those useful for large-format photography. To thoroughly understand the evolution of lenses, you must know about the constraints and obstacles all lens designers have to face. If you are not ready to investigate lens choices in depth, you may wish to begin by skimming the second part of this chapter, turning to the first section for reference whenever a term or phrase is unfamiliar.

The Anatomy of a Lens

A lens made from a single piece of glass is called a *simple lens*. Its faces may be concave, convex, or flat, but it must have at least one curved surface. This surface is almost always a *spheric section*, a surface that looks as though it were a disc sliced from the surface of a perfect sphere. Imagine, for example, a coin-sized disc cut from the skin of an orange. This piece and the same diameter disc cut from a larger sphere such as a basketball would both be spheric sections, but the latter would have a flatter surface, due to its greater *radius of curvature*. A lens that can focus an image is called a *convergent* or *positive* lens, and to do so it must be thicker in the center than at the edges. The reason a lens

can focus an image is because the glass *refracts*, or bends, light passing through it. The amount of refraction depends on the angle the light makes with the glass surface and also on the *refractive index*, a measure of the light-bending power of a specific kind of glass.

A simple, convergent lens distorts the image it produces in a number of predictable

The three shapes of convergent lenses are, from left to right, biconvex, plano-convex, and positive meniscus.

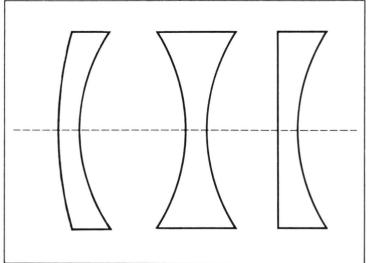

The divergent lens elements, used only in combination with positive elements, are negative meniscus, biconcave, and plano-concave.

ways. These distortions, known as *aberrations*, may be separated into seven broad categories (described on pp. 114–117), and have been well known to lens designers since the early nineteenth century. Lens aberrations can be corrected, or at least diminished, by adding other simple lenses into the light path. For example, a *divergent* (or *negative*) lens, which is thinnest in its center, is used only in combination with a convergent lens to correct an aberration. A set of simple lenses assembled along a common optical axis to focus an image forms a *compound lens*. The simple lenses are then referred to as *elements* or *components*, and may be cemented together into *groups*. Any air space between elements and groups is as important to the design of a compound lens as the elements themselves, and a fixed position of the elements and spaces is assured by a rigid lens *barrel*, its opaque outer shell. In a compound lens, a single element isolated by air spaces is also considered a group. Your normal lens probably has six elements in four groups.

Cardinal Points and Principal Planes

A lens is born in the imagination of a designer who tests out on paper each new theoretical arrangement of elements and groups by calculating the paths of different light rays through them. This *ray tracing* involves incredibly tedious and complicated calculations, and progress in lens design was predictably slow until the advent of the computer. The past three decades have seen remarkable advances in lens quality because these calculations can now be done much more rapidly, thus allowing designers to more thoroughly investigate possible arrangement variations.

Ray tracings, like most optical measurements, help define and make use of the *cardinal points* and *principal planes* of the lens. These are the various spatial positions of optical importance in a lens, some of which are defined here. By convention, diagrams are drawn showing points of light originating at the left of a lens coming to a focus on the right.

The plane slicing through the points on the left is the *object plane*, and the plane through the focused point on the right is the *image plane*. Some rays of light will leave a lens traveling parallel to the direction they entered, although displaced. The *forward nodal point* is the point on the optical axis at which all such rays entering the lens are aimed. They exit as though they emanated from the *rear nodal point*. The rear nodal point is the most important cardinal point for the user because it is from there that focal length is measured, and because any rotation of the lens around that point (as in a lens swing or tilt) will leave the position of the image plane unchanged.

The relative position of the rear nodal point defines three categories of lenses. The rear nodal point is within the lens for *normal* designs, in front of the lens for a *telephoto* design, and behind for a *retrofocus*. This means the telephoto lens itself is closer to the film than its focal length when focused at infinity, and the retrofocus is farther away. Remember, the focal length is measured from the

The plane on the left, perpendicular to the optical axis and passing through all the points in focus, is the object plane. Every point in the object plane is focused by the lens to a point in the image plane on the right.

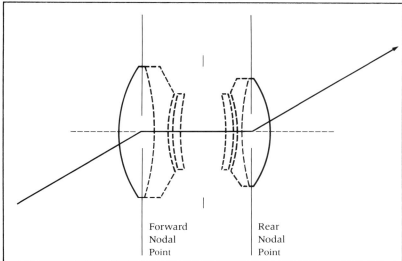

Any ray of light that leaves the lens in a path parallel to its original direction seems to enter aimed at the forward nodal point and leave from the rear nodal point. The position of the rear nodal point is very important to view camera users.

nodal point to the film. With a hand camera, having the rear nodal point farther from the film than is the lens makes a telephoto lens more compact. Having the rear nodal point closer to the film than with a normal design lens in a retrofocus makes it possible to use a short focal-length (wide-angle) lens on a reflex camera where a normal design lens of the same focal length would interfere with the reflex mirror. Because view cameras offer few physical obstructions to the use of very long and very short lenses, retrofocus lenses are never used with them and telephotos are used very rarely.

The Lens Aberrations

Ideally, a lens should cover a wide field (make a large image circle) with a sharp, evenly illuminated image, and should do so for any object distance. Aberrations make these goals impossible to accomplish simultaneously, and every lens design is a controlled compromise. Correcting for one aberration often aggravates another. The designer uses the number and shapes of elements and the optical behavior of different kinds of glass to control aberrations, and has to juggle all of the characteristics of a lens to *optimize* it for a certain use. For example, a process lens used in the graphic arts sacrifices sharpness at infinity for high performance at close range, and

gains good color correction at the expense of wide coverage.

Spherical Aberration. Light rays originating at one object point and refracted, or redirected, by a spheric surface are not, as we would like them to be, all focused at exactly the same image point. Light from the edges of a lens comes to a focus in a shorter distance than light from the central portion, and

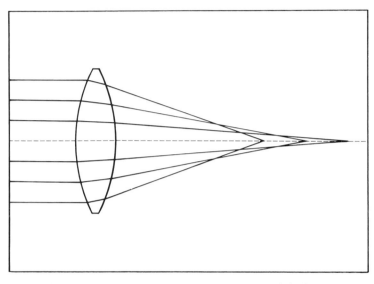

Spherical Aberration. *The rays from the periphery of the lens come to a focus closer than those passing through its center.*

This photograph was made by Dutch photographer Hans Pielage. Light passing through a homemade plastic lens clearly reveals spherical abberation.

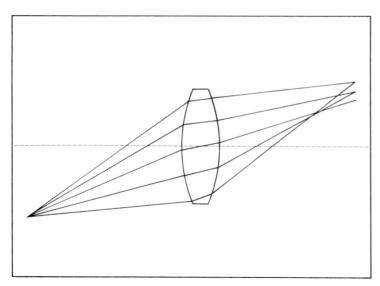

Coma. This aberration makes points of light appear to blur outward, away from the optical axis.

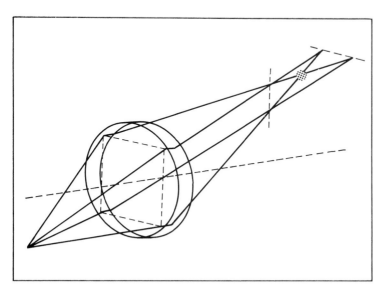

Astigmatism. A lens evidencing this aberration changes its focus with the orientation of the subject.

the farther the part of the lens refracting the light is from the lens axis (center), the more the focus strays. A simple lens exhibiting this *spherical aberration* performs better at small apertures, which restrict the light from the periphery of the lens. But trying to correct spherical aberration simply by stopping down also changes the position of the image plane. This is called a *focus shift*. The spherical aberration for any lens increases (and image quality decreases) as the object distance decreases. A lens designed for close-up work, then, must have much less residual spherical aberration than one designed for landscapes.

Spherical aberration can be controlled, but not eliminated, by adding a divergent lens to the light path. The ideal solution to the problem would be to change the spheric-section curvature of the lens surface, but only recently have mass production techniques been developed for curved surfaces of non-spherical shape. The production of the *aspheric* lens of Polaroid's SX-70 in 1972 was a manufacturing breakthrough which may lead to better view camera lenses in the future.

Coma. *Coma* is a blurring of the image in the direction of the edge. It is caused by an increase in magnification for light passing through the lens at an increased distance from the optical axis. The image of an off-axis point of light takes on the shape of a comet, hence the name. Because its effects increase with distance from the optical axis, it is a particular problem for wide-field lenses. Coma can be controlled somewhat by the designer with the position of the diaphragm. A smaller aperture reduces the problem.

Astigmatism. A lens evidencing *astigmatism* may show horizontal lines in focus while vertical lines are out of focus. Shaping a lens to correct spherical aberration often aggravates astigmatism. The first anastigmatic lenses, in which the aberration was corrected, were made after the development of barium crown glass in 1886 gave designers a wider choice of refractive indexes.

Field Curvature. *Field curvature* prevents the image of a flat object plane from lying entirely on the flat film plane. Instead, the image is focused on a curved surface. This is an especially significant problem in enlarging and in process lenses that are ordinarily used to image a flat surface, but field curvature can also make ground-glass focusing difficult if sufficiently present in a general-purpose camera lens.

Distortion. Six of the seven aberrations primarily affect the ability of a lens to focus an image precisely. *Distortion* affects its ability to focus an image accurately. To help visualize this distinction, a dirty mirror cannot make a precise image, and a curved mirror cannot make an image that is accurate. *Pincushion* and *barrel* distortion are characterized by a curving of the image that increases away from the optical axis. They are more of a problem in telephoto and retrofocus designs than they are in *symmetrical* lens designs where the elements in front and back of the diaphragm are mirror images (or nearly so) of each other. Distortion is less of a problem if it appears in a landscape lens than in one used for graphic arts, enlarging, architecture, or aerial mapping. It is unaffected by aperture.

Axial Chromatic Aberration. *Axial chromatic aberration* is a change in focus proportional to the color (wavelength) of light. Uncorrected, this aberration causes the longer wavelengths, such as red and yellow, to be focused behind the shorter blue and green wavelengths. Your eyes' chromatic aberration causes the perceptual effect (used to great advantage by many painters) that warm colors seem to advance while cool colors seem to recede. Axial chromatic aberration will cause colored fringes in a color photograph, and general unsharpness in black-and-white. The two chromatic aberrations, axial and *transverse*, are more noticeable in color photography than in black-and-white.

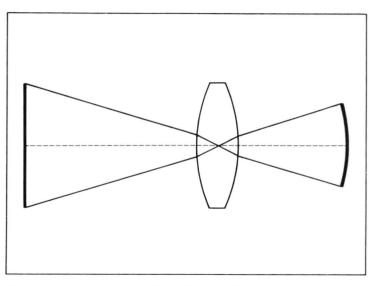

Field Curvature. *Without a flat field, it is difficult to get a sharp photograph on all parts of a flat sheet of film.*

Barrel distortion and pincushion distortion are the two common ways a lens can render an inaccurate image. The distortion increases with the distance from the optical axis.

Barrel Distortion   *Pincushion Distortion*

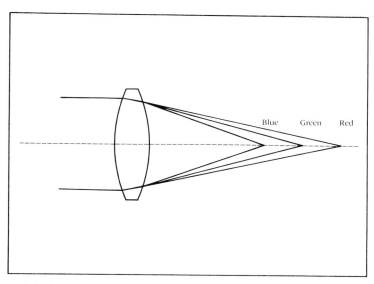

Axial Chromatic Aberration. *The lens changes its focal length slightly with the wavelength of light.*

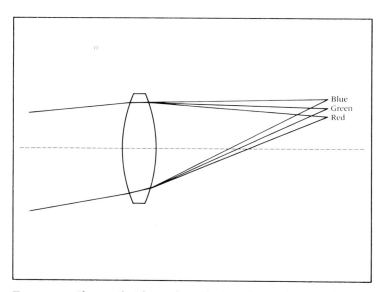

Transverse Chromatic Aberration. *The lens changes its magnification slightly with the wavelength of light.*

Lateral Color. *Transverse chromatic aberration*, also called *lateral color*, is a particular problem in long focal-length lenses of normal design (that is, not telephoto); therefore, it affects most process lenses. Lateral color causes the focal length of the lens to change with wavelength, which produces colored fringes on color film. The printing industry uses three black-and-white *color-separation* negatives to reproduce a color photograph. If these negatives are shot with a lens exhibiting transverse chromatic aberration, the images on the separations will be of different sizes and the resulting reproduction will be out of focus.

Other Lens Imperfections

As you have seen by now, no lens is perfect. The materials used to make lenses have properties that work against us. Aberrations are not the only undesirable properties that must be minimized by the designer and side-stepped by the cautious user; a few others are discussed below.

Flare. One undesirable property of the glass used in lenses is its tendency to transmit less than 100 percent of the light that falls on it. Some of the light, usually not much, is reflected back toward its source. Every surface of the lens transmits most of the light and reflects some, and some of the light reflected forward from the rear elements is reflected back again by the back surface of the front elements. This stray reflected light, called *flare*, is not focused into an image, but serves only to reduce contrast when it falls upon the film. Lower contrast reduces apparent sharpness and degrades the image.

A cemented surface between glass elements reflects about 1 percent and transmits 99 percent of any light falling on it. A glass-air surface, however, reflects as much as 6 percent, and a compound lens can have eight such surfaces. Fortunately, a practical method to apply an antireflection coating (by vacuum deposition) was introduced in 1935, and the light loss in a well-designed compound lens was reduced to a total of less than 6 percent. Recent techniques in multiple coating have reduced total flare below 1 percent, and new multicoated lenses are available for view cameras. Reduced reflection gives the lens designer freedom to use more elements in correcting aberrations.

Although controlled by coating, lens flare is aggravated by other sources of stray light, such as reflections from poorly darkened shutter and diaphragm blades, lens barrel, bellows, and internal camera parts. Even the surface of the film reflects as much as 20 percent of the light falling on it, which can be reflected back by the interior of the bellows and the rear of the lens and lensboard. Any surface imperfections on the lens such as chips, scratches, dust, or fingermarks, or light falling on the front of the lens from outside the subject area, will scatter light and contribute to flare. To minimize image degradation due to flare, keep your lenses clean and dust-free, and shade the lens during exposure. Remember that using a lens with much more coverage than you need only produces troublesome extra light which must be absorbed by the bellows.

Diffraction. Light behaves in some ways like rays, or like beams of atomic particles, and in some ways like waves. One form of behavior best explained by a wave theory is that of light striking the edge of an object. The edge of the diaphragm, for example, causes the light striking it to *diffract*, or spread, in an unfocused way similar to flare, resulting in decreased contrast and resolution. Since it only happens at an edge, the extent to which it affects the image depends upon the proportion of edge light to center light. Mathematically, the circumference of the diaphragm, its edge, is a multiple of its diameter; in other words, the circumference is directly proportional to the radius. The total amount of light transmitted through a circular opening depends upon its area, which is proportional to the *square* of the radius. This means that as the aperture size increases, the area will increase at a greater rate than the circumference, and the proportion of diffracted light will decrease. Diffraction is therefore only a problem of smaller apertures.

In practice, stopping down a lens increases sharpness by reducing residual spherical aberration and coma until the diffraction begins to reduce image quality at the very small apertures. The middle apertures of any lens are the ones that have the best combination of reduced residual aberration and diffraction with increased coverage and evenness of illumination and definition.

Field Illumination. Four different factors inhibit the ability of a lens to produce an evenly illuminated image across its entire covering circle, or field. First, the inverse square law tells us that illumination of a subject diminishes with the square of its distance

Schneider makes this graduated neutral-density filter to correct uneven field illumination in their wide-field lenses.

from the light source. Since the lens functions as the light source for the film, and the center of the film is closest to the lens, the illumination of the film will diminish toward the edges.

Second, for light entering the lens at an angle, the aperture is an ellipse rather than the circle it appears to be for light entering along the optical axis. As the angle away from the axis increases, the ellipse gets smaller in area. Again, this effect diminishes the illumination given the film in proportion to the distance from its center.

Third, for the same reason that the noon-day sun is the hottest, any light that reaches the film at an angle loses intensity in proportion to that angle, resulting yet again in less illumination at the edges of the film.

Fourth, vignetting (or shading) by the lens barrel causes a difference in illumination between the center and edges of the field, resulting in diminished illumination away from the center.

The effects of these four factors compound each other and work against the designer, who is trying to produce a lens with an evenly illuminated field. It might seem to be a losing battle. Despite all these obstacles, however, uneven field illumination can be manageable, even inconsequential, with small field angles. Unfortunately, uneven illumination increases greatly with large field angles and becomes a significant problem in the design and use of wide-angle lenses. The introduction of extremely large lens elements in modern wide-field designs has helped to reduce vignetting, and the use of smaller apertures improves uneven illumination considerably. But even the best wide-field lenses still show a noticeable exposure variation from center to edges.

Fortunately for wide-angle lens users, a photograph slightly lighter in its center than at its edges is aesthetically more comfortable than the reverse. And often, uneven illumination in an enlarger will compensate by being brighter in the center, where the uneven negative is most dense. Dependable correction of an uneven field can be assured by adding to the front of the lens a special neutral-colored filter graduated with increasing density from the edges to the center. These filters are available from Schneider in sizes for their Super-Angulon series of wide-angle lenses and cost almost as much as the lenses they fit. They can be adapted to fit the fronts of other lenses.

A History of Lens Design

Each of today's view-camera lenses is a member of a family, a descendant of well-documented nineteenth-century ancestors. Because the performance characteristics of a lens — contrast, sharpness, color correction, and coverage — are often predictable if you know its lineage, we will trace the development of photographic optics up to the establishment of the major lens design families. Now that you are familiar with the problems and constraints of the lens designer's job, you can read this lens genealogy and investigate some possible lens choices for your own use.

Most nineteenth-century lenses are now only collector's items, generally inadequate for use by today's standards of optical quality. Until the 1950s, each new generation of lens designs was accompanied by significant advances in quality. Since then, with the advent of antireflection coating and computer design, we have seen not revolution but refinement. Since most of the postwar lenses can be considered viable for your use, many of the more common models you might find for sale secondhand will be introduced in this section. After you have read the design history, the section following it on current lenses organized by their family trees will help you know the strengths and weaknesses of the available modern lenses based on their origins.

Origin and Development

The first improvement over the pinhole as a lens was developed for the *camera obscura* (the camera's antecedent), and resulted from the use of the simplest forms of a single-element glass lens. The *biconvex* lens is a plain "burning glass" with convex faces on both sides (the word *lens*, in fact, is Latin for lentil, a biconvex legume). In a camera obscura, a glass biconvex lens greatly increased the intensity of light at the focal plane for a much brighter image than a pinhole could form. Because the biconvex is thicker in the center than the edges, it is a positive lens and causes light rays to converge to a focus. From the introduction of this simple lens, the history of lenses is a sequence of attempts to reduce its aberrations.

The biconvex lens suffers from such extreme chromatic and spherical aberration that it can be used only with very small apertures, and then only for a very small field angle. A *plano-convex* lens, one with one face flat and the other convex, reduces the spherical aberration somewhat. To improve the performance of the camera obscura, a positive *meniscus* lens, with one face convex and the

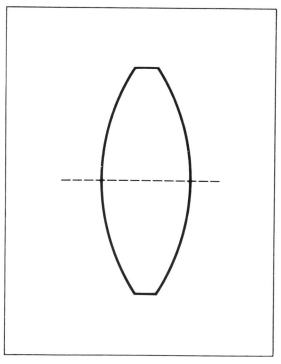

The simple "burning glass" biconvex lens was the first improvement over the pinhole in the development of camera lenses.

The plano-convex simple lens has somewhat less spherical and chromatic aberration than the biconvex.

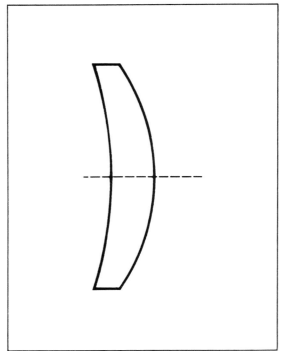

Wollaston devised a positive meniscus in 1812 for an improvement in astigmatism and coma over the plano-convex lens.

other concave, was devised by British physicist William Hyde Wollaston in 1812. This shape reduces astigmatism and coma and provides the best compromise of aberrations available in a simple lens. The meniscus has been in continuous production for the entire history of photography for inexpensive box and folding cameras.

The Compound Lens. The Giroux Daguerreotype camera of 1839, the first camera to be produced in multiples, used a meniscus lens made by Charles Chevalier, with an aperture of about f/15. Chevalier's meniscus was formed by cementing a negative biconcave element to a biconvex. This group was positioned behind the diaphragm. Its overall shape was a positive meniscus so it would still bring an image to a focus. This lens introduced an additional element to control aberrations and was therefore the first successful compound lens for any camera. The two cemented elements were made of different kinds of glass selected to introduce color shifts in opposite directions that cancelled each other, thus removing much of the chromatic aberration. Called *achromatic* for this reduced aberration, lenses of this design also became known as *Landscape* lenses.

The next major step in the development of the modern lens was taken by Josef Petzval, in Vienna, who designed a lens in 1840 by mathematically calculating its behavior before it was constructed. Not only was it the first time this technique had been applied to a photographic lens, but it was the first lens Petzval had designed and it turned out to be a milestone.

Petzval made this compound lens, commissioned for the all-metal Voigtländer camera of 1841, from a cemented two-element achromatic meniscus by adding opposite the diaphragm two elements separated by an air space. It was the sharpest lens then available, and at f/3.6 was almost twenty times faster than the meniscus lenses of the day. Sitting for a portrait in this era meant having one's head clamped still for the duration of a exposure that might last 30 seconds, and any increase in the speed of a lens was welcomed by photographers and subjects alike. With a covering angle of only about 20°, the Petzval lens could not be considered normal (a lens must have a covering angle of about 52° for the diameter of the covering circle to equal the focal length), but because portrait photographers usually prefer to use a longer than

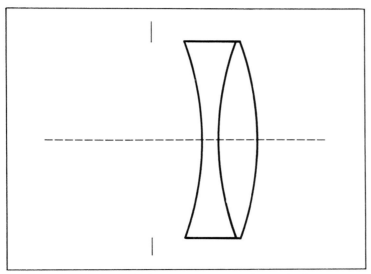

Chevalier's meniscus, made for Daguerre's camera, was the first success-ful compound lens.

Petzval lens

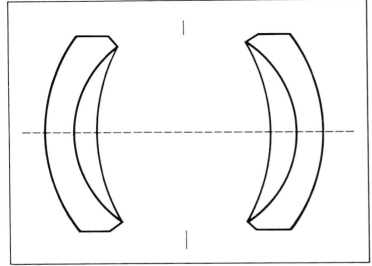

Aplanat or Rapid Rectilinear

normal lens, the narrow coverage proved not to be a limitation. The Petzval design became the standard portrait lens for more than sixty years.

The Symmetrical Lens Family. The 1860s saw the emergence of the first *symmetrical* lens designs. When two identical lenses or groups are mounted as mirror images around a central diaphragm, the three transverse aberrations — lateral color, distortion, and coma — will be positive for one side and negative for the other. These aberrations of opposite orientation act to reduce each other, leaving the designer free to concentrate on reducing the other four aberrations. The reduction of the three transverse aberrations is at its maximum at 1:1 reproduction; when object distance and image distance are equal the transverse aberrations totally cancel each other out.

In 1866, Munich's Steinheil introduced the *Aplanat* and Dallmeyer of London the *Rapid Rectilinear.* In these first successful symmetrical designs, a two-element achromatic meniscus was designed to suppress chromatic and spherical aberration. This compound lens was then used for both the front and rear groups around a diaphragm that was positioned to reduce astigmatism. These lenses covered a field of 50° at f/8 with excellent definition, and were free of distortion. This *rectilinear* design (no curvilinear distortion) dramatically improved architectural photographs. Prior to these early symmetrical designs, distortion was always noticeable in photographs of linear objects.

Despite the improvements brought by these rectilinear lenses, including significant reduction of several aberrations, astigmatism was still noticeably present, and field curvature limited the maximum aperture. The ingredients needed to bring these problems under control were developed by Dr. Otto Schott of Jena, in what is now East Germany. Beginning in 1884, his four-year investigations into new optical glass types gave lens designers the key to reducing astigmatism and flattening the field. *Anastigmatic* lenses were the next leap forward.

Before Schott's experiments, opticians and lens designers were limited to using *crown* glass, a high-quality plate glass, and *flint* glass, made by adding lead. By adding other materials such as barium and zinc to the basic crown formula, the glass works at Jena produced new glasses with a wider range of refractive index and made possible the first anastigmat, the *Ross Concentric*. Patented in 1888, the Concentric showed improved performance from its reduced astigmatism, but its maximum aperture of f/16 made it too slow for practical use. The Concentric was rapidly eclipsed by the *Double Anastigmat*. Designed in 1892 by Emil von Höegh and manufactured by C. P. Goerz of Berlin, the Double Anastigmat had symmetrical front and rear groups each made of three cemented elements and it covered a field of 60° at f/6.8. After 1904, the Double Anastigmat became known as the *Dagor*, and lenses of this formula are still being produced.

In Jena, Carl Zeiss produced a lens similar to the Dagor, called the *Double Protar*, which was designed as a *convertible* lens. Each half of the lens comprised four cemented elements and could be separated and used independently. The four-element halves themselves had different focal lengths, and connecting them resulted in a third. In theory, the photographer could have the utility of three lenses by owning one. Unfortunately, since much of the correction for aberrations provided by a symmetrical lens depends upon balancing positive error from one group with negative error from the other, the optical performance of the individual groups in a convertible lens is usually well below that of the complete lens.

Three important variants of the cemented symmetrical lens were introduced around the turn of the century. By separating one of the three elements in each of the two groups by introducing an air space, the six-element Double Anastigmat design became the four-

Double Anastigmat

Double Protar

This Busch Vademacum is a convertible lens set made in Germany about 1900. Interchanging elements resulted in seven different focal lengths.

Planar

Plasmat

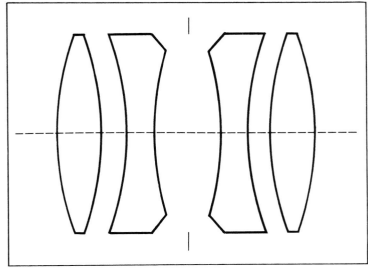

Celor

group *Plasmat* of Hugo Meyer and the Zeiss *Planar*. The former has an air space surrounding the inner two elements, and the latter has the outer elements mounted singly. Also, the Plasmat uses negative groups on the outside and positive groups inside, while the Planar has its convergent groups on the outside. The Schneider *Symmar* (the predecessor to the current Symmar-S) was a convertible (three focal lengths) Plasmat. In 1898 Von Höegh made a four-element lens in which each half was an achromat meniscus with its two elements separated by an air space. This was the Goerz *Celor* f/4.5, later the *Dogmar*. Like the Planar, the Celor's outer elements are convergent, the inner ones divergent.

The basic concept of the symmetrical lens has continued to evolve and improve. The *Opic*, an f/2 lens of the Planar type produced in the 1920s by Taylor, Taylor and Hobson in England, began a design trend by showing that coma correction could be improved by making the front group larger than the rear. Although not strictly symmetrical, lenses of this type are still considered part of the symmetrical lens family. The Planar, Plasmat, and Celor designs are used as the basis for most of today's normal lenses for large-format photography.

The Triplet Family. A large family of lenses can trace its ancestry to the *Cooke* lens, introduced by Taylor, Taylor and Hobson in 1893. The Cooke was the first successful *triplet* lens, one whose elements form three distinct groups. The earliest triplet had been made in 1860 by Dallmeyer, but was displaced by the successful Rapid Rectilinear, which offered less distortion. The Cooke gained popularity, however, because of its good performance, low price, and wide f/4.5 aperture.

The most successful triplet design was calculated in 1902 by Paul Rudolph for Zeiss. Similar to the Cooke lens, Rudolph's *Tessar* substituted a cemented pair for the Cooke's single rear element, which flattened the field and improved spherical aberration. For its fast maximum aperture of f/4.5, the Tessar was the best corrected lens available at the time. Kodak's later *Ektar* and *Commercial Ektar* were popular Tessar-formula lenses.

Wide-Field Lenses. Very early experiments into wide-field design included an 1859 water-filled globe lens covering 120° and a 1900 lens incorporating a spinning propeller. The first well-corrected wide-field lenses appeared after the turn of the century based on the symmetrical *Gauss* design. The ancestor of these lenses was a pair of meniscus-shaped elements used as a telescope objective, designed by German mathematician K. F. Gauss. Hugo Meyer introduced the Gauss design as a photographic lens called the *Aristostigmat*, a symmetrical lens having two pairs of meniscus single elements. Many wide-field lenses from the recent past, including Kodak's popular *Wide-Field Ektar*, were similar four-element Gauss designs. Most of the modern wide-field lenses are derived from the Gauss formula, but have more than four elements.

Some early improvements in Gauss wide-field designs resulted in six-element, two group lenses, such as the Goerz *Wide-Angle Dagor*, a version of the Double Anastigmat.

Cooke Triplet

This cutaway section of a real lens reveals the accurate nature of schematic drawings.

Tessar

Gauss lens (Aristostigmat)

Wide-Angle Dagor

Schneider Angulon

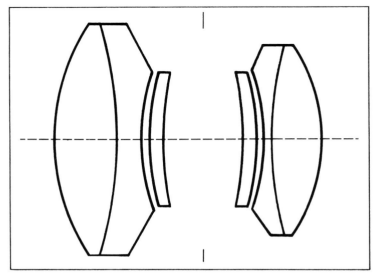

Nikkor-W

All wide-field lenses for view cameras are symmetrical designs with variations on the order of the elements and the inclusion of air spaces. The W. A. Dagor uses two groups, each with a negative element cemented between two positive components. The similar Schneider *Angulon* f/6.8, introduced in 1930, has a convergent element cemented between two divergent components. Like the W. A. Dagor, the Angulon is a well-corrected, compact lens. It covers a field of 85° and is readily available secondhand in focal lengths from 65 to 210mm. As with the Gauss-formula wide-angle lenses the maximum aperture in either of these two lenses is useful only for focusing because the field is only well corrected below f/16.

Modern Lens Designs

Symmetrical Designs. Lenses of symmetrical design in all focal lengths dominate today's available lens choices. If you wish to begin with a good all-purpose lens, a Plasmat design of near normal focal length should be your choice. Most have a maximum aperture of f/5.6, which under most circumstances is certainly wide enough to provide a bright image for focusing. The covering angle for a Plasmat, usually 60° at full aperture, increases to 70° at f/22. Schneider's *Symmar-S*, the Nikkor *W*, the Fujinon *NWS*, and Calumet's *Caltar-S* are f/5.6 Plasmats with the front group slightly larger than the rear. The Fujinon *AS* and Computar *f/9 Convertible* are totally symmetrical but slower. Most of today's Plasmats are made in a range of focal lengths from 100mm to 360mm. The Symmar-S is also available in 480mm, and the Fuji AS has been made in 600 and 1200mm. A 150mm Plasmat will project a covering circle with a diameter greater than 200mm at f/22 — large enough for 5x7, or for 4x5 with lots of room for movements.

Similar in performance to the Plasmats is Rodenstock's *Sironar-N*, an f/5.6 Planar type with enlarged front element. These lenses are available from 100 to 360mm. Schneider's *Xenotar* is a five-element Planar design, covering 56°. Three focal lengths are made, but only the longest, 150mm, is suitable for 4x5. Compared to the Plasmats, the Xenotar's coverage is limited, but a maximum aperture of f/2.8 makes the lens desirable for any low-light or high-speed application.

The turn-of-the-century Celor four-element design is still popular as a process lens. Rodenstock's *Apo-Ronar*, the Schneider

Apo-Artar, and its forerunner, the Goerz *Red Dot Artar*, are Celor designs optimized for reproduction ratios near 1:1. These lenses are also carefully corrected for the three *process* colors (cyan, magenta, and yellow — used to reproduce color photographs in print) and therefore cannot simultaneously be well corrected for a large aperture or wide field. Fortunately, process cameras are focused by distance scales so a wide aperture for visual focusing is unnecessary, and the narrow covering angle is not a problem because the long image distance resulting from near 1:1 reproduction produces a much larger image circle than these same lenses would at infinity focus. But maximum apertures no greater than f/9 and field angles around 45° usually prevent their use on anything other than process cameras. A lens like these Celor derivatives with careful three-color correction is called an *Apochromat*.

Triplets. Rodenstock's economical *Geronar* keeps the Triplet family alive. It is a classic 1893 three-element Cooke formula lens and is available in 210 and 300mm versions. Another Cooke Triplet is the Fujinon *SF*, a controlled-soft-focus lens. Like Rodenstock's *Imagon* (even more anachronistic than the Geronar, it is a two-element achromatic meniscus), the SF is designed to introduce controlled aberrations for a soft-focus effect and is produced mainly for portrait photographers.

Rudolph's classic Tessar formula lives on in the current Schneider *Xenar*, Nikkor-*M*, Fujinon *LS*, and Caltar *Pro*. Covering 50 to 60°, they are an alternative to the Plasmats for a general-purpose lens if your applications require few movements or a longer-than-normal focal length. The four-element Tessar has fewer surfaces to generate flare than the six-element Plasmat and will therefore usually produce a higher-contrast image.

Wide-Field Lenses. All wide-field lenses made today for view cameras are symmetrical designs. Although current symmetrical lens designs for normal lenses are little different from their progenitors, wide-field lenses have benefited from great improvement. Reducing aberrations is much more difficult for wider-field angles, and the introduction of additional elements to control these aberrations has always been inhibited by the additional flare that would result from extra reflecting surfaces. The greatest benefit of recently developed multicoating techniques has been to those lenses with many ele-

Schneider Xenotar

Rodenstock Apo-Ronar

Fujinon-LS or Schneider Xenar

Barbara Crane made this photograph of the staircase to the Chicago Public Library's Preston Bradley Hall in 1976. With her wide-field lens, she used a front rise to keep the columns vertical while the view seems to be looking up the stairs.

ments: zoom lenses (not made for large-format cameras) and lenses with extremely wide fields. Designers are now free to use as many as eight elements to produce a well-corrected wide field without loss of illumination or image degradation from flare. The only drawback is cost; modern wide-field view-camera lenses are among the most expensive pieces of professional gear. But for the working photographer whose reputation depends on an image of quality, today's wide-field lenses are a godsend.

The first truly modern wide-field lens for large-format was the Schneider *Super-Angulon* f/8, introduced in 1956. Available in focal lengths from 65 to 210 mm, this six-element symmetrical lens design has a useful field angle of 100°. The Fujinon *NSWS* has the same design and much the same performance. The longest focal length of the Fuji wide angles, now discontinued, was the immense (weighing over three kilograms) 300mm. At f/22, the 300 covered a 720mm circle, big enough for 18x22-inch film.

A 1966 addition to Schneider's wide-field line is the *Series II f/5.6 Super Angulon*, with eight elements and a 105° field. Available in focal lengths from 47 to 90mm, these lenses are larger, heavier, and more expensive than the f/8 versions. But in addition to ease of viewing and focusing from the additional stop of brightness, improvements are apparent in field illumination and sharpness at the edges of the image circle. The Rodenstock *Grandagon* f/4.5 has the same design and performance, and is almost a full stop faster. Nikon's *SW* f/8 lenses, in 90 and 120mm, are also the same design and offer the same performance, although they are slower.

A curious asymmetrical eight-element design marks Fuji's premium *SWDS* f/5.6 lenses: 65, 75, and 90mm. At f/22 they cover 105°. Nikon's *SW* series also includes an unusual asymmetrical design. With seven elements in four groups for the 65mm f/4 and the 75 and 90mm f/4.5, these lenses reach 105° at f/16. None of these lenses, or any wide-angle lens for that matter, should be used for photographing at its maximum aperture. The ground glass will be almost four times as bright for focusing and viewing with an f/4.5 lens as with an f/8, but in both cases only the center of the image is usable at the widest aperture. The Nikon indicates a significant design advancement, reaching optimum performance at f/16 instead of the usual f/22.

Schneider Super-Angulon

Nikkor-SW

This 165mm wide-field Super-Angulon dwarfs a modern 35mm camera. The large lens is a wide-angle when used with 8x10 film.

Jim Dow makes contact prints from the 8x10 color negatives he takes with his Deardorff camera and wide-field lens. This is Dow's Rear Display Room, Dyson's Jewellers, Leeds, West Yorkshire, England, 1983. *Original in color.*

Arch Construction III, Moscone Site, 1981, *by San Francisco's Catherine Wagner, documented that city's construction of a new convention center with a 90mm wide-field lens of her 4x5 field camera. A short focal length wide-field lens is a necessity when working in an area like this with severely restricted vantage points.*

The anachronism of the available wide-field lenses, Rodenstock's economical 90mm f/8 *Geronar WA*, is a four-element Aristostigmat (Gauss-type) formula from 1900. Perhaps the only such design available for view cameras, its 85° field makes it only barely useful as a wide-angle for 4x5.

Wide-field lenses for view cameras, despite their shortcomings, have a distinct advantage in their symmetrical design over the retrofocus wide-angles necessary for single-lens reflex cameras. The mirror that must be interposed between lens and film in a SLR requires the use of a wide-angle lens whose *back focus* (or image distance at infinity focus) is longer than its focal length. A retrofocus lens (sometimes called an inverted, or reversed, telephoto) cannot be made with a symmetrical design. The quality of such a lens suffers because it is much more difficult to correct, requires more elements, and is more expensive to manufacture than a symmetrical design of equal focal length and coverage. If you are accustomed to using wide lenses on small cameras, you will be very pleased to see how much better the optical quality can be from using a wide lens on a view camera.

When Jim Dow's 165mm Super-Angulon lens doesn't provide a large enough angle of view, he carefully pieces together three prints from the same vantage point, as here: Reading Room, The British Library, Bloomsbury, London, 1983. *This photograph, like the one on page 129, shows Dow's use of the descriptive powers of a large-format photograph to reveal a precise, detailed catalog of everything that was visible to the lens (original in color).*

8 Accessories and Options

In addition to your camera, lens, and shutter, you will need or may want to use a number of accessories. Most large-format cameras cannot be used without a tripod, hand-held light meter, and cable release, all of which are considered advanced options in the use of smaller cameras. As with lenses, these and other accessories are invariably manufactured by a different company from the one that made your camera, giving you the pleasure of a wide range of choices but also the responsibility of ensuring that each accessory is compatibile with the rest of your equipment and suitable for your needs.

This chapter discusses camera stands, light meters, and other items not supplied with the view camera, and includes further information about some accessories already discussed, such as film holders. The last section of the chapter describes those parts of your camera, such as the bellows, ground glass, and lensboard, for which options are available from your camera's manufacturer. With all these options and accessories you can tailor the versatile view camera exactly to your specific personal or professional photographic needs.

Accessories

Camera Stands

Few large-format cameras were designed to be used hand-held. The longer focal-length lenses necessary to cover large sheets of film require smaller apertures for adequate depth of field, and small apertures require shutter speeds too slow for the camera to be held steadily. The few large cameras designed for hand-held use were a poor compromise in an era that gave the photographer no satisfactory options. Back then, if you couldn't get the picture with a large-format camera, you didn't get the picture. Today, with high-quality 35mm equipment satisfying any need for speed and portability, your reasons for using large-format equipment probably do not include any good excuses for hand-held work.

You will also find it impossible to learn to use the camera or control its movements if it is not held still for you. The first accessory for you to consider, then, is a camera stand to get the camera out of your hands.

Tripods. The most common camera stand is a *tripod*, which consists of three legs joined at their tops with a platform to support the camera. Like the early cameras, the tripods that held them were made of wood. Surveyors still use wooden tripods to support their optical equipment because the wood construction makes them resistant to binding caused by dust and dirt. The few wooden tripods still made for cameras are particularly useful for work in the field around dirt or water.

Most camera tripods currently available are aluminum, with tubular legs and a cast

The shorter tripod is more compact but requires more time to set up. Both will place a camera at about the same maximum height.

Some tripods allow the center column to be reversed for low-angle photographs.

A large, heavy, professional tripod should be equipped with a geared crank on the center column to make vertical adjustments with a heavy camera easier.

platform. An aluminum tripod can be adjusted more precisely and easily and is much lighter than a similar wooden one. Each tubular leg is made of concentric segments that can be extended independently and locked in place. The number of leg segments is a compromise between portability and maximum height. Unless you need an extremely compact tripod for portability, or one taller than you, three-segment legs should be sufficient. Setting up and collapsing a tripod with four- or five-segment legs can be time consuming and tedious.

Most tripods have an extendable center column to allow easy vertical adjustments and to increase the maximum height permitted by the legs alone. For heavy cameras, this center column should be geared and have a crank handle to raise and lower the camera. A reversible center column allows you to suspend the camera below the tripod for low-angle shots. Increasing the height of the camera with the center column rather than by extending the legs makes the camera less stable, so use the center column only for small adjustments in height.

Conventional wisdom dictates that your tripod should weigh at least as much as your camera so it can resist vibration from air movement and provide a solid base of support. The larger the diameter of the leg segments, the more the tripod has of both stability and weight. If you must use a lightweight tripod in the field, you can increase its resistance to wind by hanging a weight or heavy bag below the center column.

Monostands. During the first century of photography, the itinerant photographer carried a tripod for camera support while his indoor counterpart used a special table. This table, with its tilting top and wheeled legs, is the direct ancestor of today's *monostand*.

Whenever portability ceases to be an issue, sturdiness is the most important attribute of a camera stand. Monostands are much heavier and consequently sturdier than tripods. A monostand is a heavy column resting on a wide, low base. A horizontal arm extends from the column to hold the camera. The arm is usually counterbalanced with weights or springs so you can move it easily up and down the column while it supports a heavy camera. Optional locking wheels on the base allow you to move the heavy monostand easily and lock its position for shooting, and you may also select arms and columns of different lengths to suit your needs. An optional accessory tray on the arm or column

A monostand is the best camera support for a view camera that stays in the studio.

A double-tilt tripod head allows easy adjustment of the camera position around three axes.

A ball head is more compact and easier to transport than a double-tilt head, but not as convenient to use.

provides a convenient resting place for film holders or a light meter. In the studio, you will probably prefer a monostand to a tripod. It adjusts more easily, occupies less floor space, and allows the camera to be positioned against or cantilevered over a tabletop surface.

Tripod Heads. All monostands, and tripods large enough to be used for view cameras, are made by suppliers of professional photographic equipment. One indication of a professional tripod is that it is sold as a set of legs independent of a support platform and its adjustment mechanism — the *tripod head*. In addition to clamping the camera firmly to the tripod or monostand, the head allows you to adjust the position of the platform and camera. You will have a choice of several different heads to fit your choice of camera stand.

Three types of tripod heads are available: single-tilt, double-tilt, and ball. *Single-tilt* heads allow adjustment only around a horizontal axis (similar to a tilt of the entire camera), and are most often used for cinema and video. They are made to *pan*, or rotate smoothly during a shot, a quality unnecessary for most still-camera work. A *double-tilt* head, the most common for still photography, provides two levers to adjust the angle of the platform around two perpendicular horizontal axes, tilting front to back and side to side. A *ball* head works much like a human shoulder joint — it is a ball-and-socket. Only a few ball-heads are sturdy enough for constant use with a view camera, but their light weight and compact construction makes them desirable for field work.

All three types of tripod head are available in different sizes, each based upon the

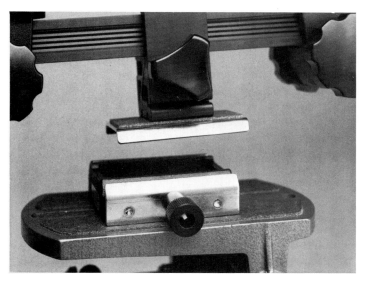

You should consider using a quick-release bracket if you need to disconnect and reconnect your camera and tripod frequently.

This twin-bracket adapter can help ease the strain that a long bellows extension and heavy camera place on the monorail.

weight of the largest camera it is expected to support. When you select a tripod head, be sure the platform is large enough for your camera, that its movements are smooth, and that it can securely lock your camera in place, even at an angle. A larger head will lock any camera more securely and its longer levers give you more control when adjusting it, but it will also weigh more and take up more room.

Your tripod head will have a threaded mounting bolt projecting through its plat-form. Make certain the threads match those of the corresponding hole in your camera's baseplate. The bolts come in two standard sizes: $\frac{1}{4}$-20 ($\frac{1}{4}$ inch diameter, 20 threads per inch) is the smaller of the two, and that thread size is used in the tripod mounting hole on most hand cameras; the larger $\frac{3}{8}$-16 is called the European thread and is safer for use with larger, heavier cameras. The camera mounting platforms on larger tripods often come with two interchangeable bolts, one in each of the standard sizes. You can buy a threaded adapter to fit the smaller bolt into the larger hole, but it makes a weaker connection than using the correct size bolt.

Tripod Adapters. If you need to connect and disconnect your camera and its tripod frequently, you might consider using an accessory two-part bracket available for rapid mounting. One part of this *quick-release* adapter couples with the camera and nests into the other part, which is held to the tripod head. The two parts then clasp or bayonet together firmly and release with the press of a button or catch. A quick-release adapter does not make as strong and secure a connection between camera and tripod as the standard mount and can fail when used with heavy cameras in unusual camera positions.

Another accessory adapter, sometimes called a *twin bracket* or *twin head*, can be handy when you use a monorail camera for extreme close-ups or with long focal-length lenses. You will find that these situations greatly increase the distance between lens and film and cause balance problems for the camera and tripod. With a large, heavy lens and a long bellows extension, you can put great strain on the monorail and tripod head. A long rail, particularly one made up of shorter sections, may be forced out of alignment inadvertently.

To compensate for the bending force on the rail, use a tripod adapter such as the one shown here to hold two rail clamps (you can buy a second rail clamp as an accessory for most monorails). Twin bracket adapters are often sold for the purpose of mounting two cameras side by side on one tripod, but one can be used to provide two points of support for the monorail instead of the usual single point. Use caution when positioning the camera, for the adapter will increase the distance between the tripod head's platform and the camera. This additional distance will raise the center of gravity of your camera and make it more difficult for the tripod head to

For extreme bellows extensions, your rail should be supported by two tripods.

hold an inclined camera. The farther from level you position the rail, the more strain there will be on the head and the greater the likelihood you will tip the entire tripod.

For extremely long extensions, or situations where a two-clamp adapter proves inadequate, you should use two tripods. Setting up a camera on two tripods is awkward, but will result in a setup unlikely to vibrate or fall.

Cable Release

A *cable release* is a flexible plunger that triggers your camera's shutter. Its tip threads into the proper fitting on your shutter, and a release button that fits your fingers caps the plunger at the other end. An internal spring returns the plunger when you stop pressing on it. You must have a cable release for most view camera operations.

Start with one about 16 inches (40cm) long. You should be able to release the shutter with your hand far enough away from the camera that you don't risk jarring it. If you cannot stand next to the camera, or for some reason need to operate the shutter from a distance, there are cable-release extensions as long as 10 meters, rubber bulb air-tube releases twice that length, timed releases, and even radio-controlled and infrared-triggered remote control releases. If your shutter has no T (for Time) setting to keep the shutter open for a longer exposure than its slowest setting, you may wish to use a locking cable release, one that can be set to remain in the extended position until you release it. Before buying any cable release, try it with your lens to make sure the tip at the shutter end extends far enough to trigger your shutter. It is not uncommon for a photographer to have a cable release for each lens, and to leave them attached during storage.

Light Meters

When you are photographing with any camera, the correct exposure for a situation is most easily determined by measuring the light intensity with a *light meter*. Most hand cameras are now equipped with built-in meters, and many amateur photographers are unaware that there is an option. With a view camera, you must use a separate light meter. Hand-held light meters are of two types: *reflected* light meters, which you point at the subject from camera position to read the light reflected from the subject, and *incident* me-

A good cable release is a necessary accessory to your view camera. For releasing the shutter from a distance, an air release is better. Air tube extensions are available.

Light meters have become more accurate and easier to use with developments in electronics. The three major types are (clockwise from the top) incident/reflected, spot, and strobe.

A probe connected to this light meter reads directly from the spot the film will be during exposure.

ters, which you point at the camera from the subject position to read the light falling on (or incident upon) the subject. Both are equally useful in the hands of an experienced photographer. Some meters are designed to measure light both ways.

Some reflected light meters are designed to read only a very narrow angle of the incoming light. These are called *spot* meters, many of which read a tiny circle at the end of an imaginary one-degree cone. Spot meters are most useful for black-and-white shooting in which tonal values of different parts of the same scene must be determined independently, such as with the Zone System. Another group of meters, mostly designed as incident-reading, can measure a short burst of light. These are called *flash* meters (or *strobe* meters) and are a tremendous help in the studio for use with electronic flash.

Designed especially for 4x5 view cameras (and for larger cameras with reducing backs) are several other meters and meter attachments that read directly from the ground-glass image. Some will read flash as well as continuous light, and all have the virtue of compensating directly for light loss due to bellows extension.

Darkcloth

Even with your lens at full aperture, the inverted image on the ground glass is too dim to be seen well without surrounding it in darkness. A *darkcloth* made from a simple one-yard (one-meter) square of black cloth can be used to cover the camera and your head simultaneously, and is sufficient to allow easy viewing. An improvement on the simple black cloth is the addition of a light-colored facing on one side. A white or silver side used facing out will reflect sunlight instead of absorbing it, and will make focusing much more comfortable on warm, sunny days. The second layer of cloth also makes the darkcloth more opaque for viewing and the light side can be used as a reflector for bouncing light into a scene. You can also use the darkcloth to wrap and protect your camera between uses.

When it's windy, keeping the cloth secure on the camera requires some ingenuity. Here are some possible solutions: fasten the darkcloth to the camera with added clips; use Velcro strips on camera and cloth; sew a circle of elastic into one end of the cloth; or tie the cloth around your neck like a cape and then secure the bottom around the ground glass with a clothespin.

Viewing Hoods

If the darkcloth seems like a burden, you might use one of a number of accessory viewing and focusing hoods that attach to the back of the camera. The simplest hoods merely replace the darkcloth with a rigid metal or plastic clip-on shade. Some, similar to a compendium, have a built-in eyepiece (sometimes a magnifying eyepiece) so that viewing admits no stray light to the back of the ground glass. More sophisticated (and expensive) are *reflex* viewers that invert the ground-glass image for right-side-up viewing of the normally upside-down image. Unfortunately, none of the accessory viewers wraps and protects your camera between uses as well as a darkcloth.

This accessory hood makes viewing easier by reinverting the image, magnifying it, and darkening the area around the ground glass.

Filters and Holders

The professional view camera user is likely to need a variety of filters for contrast control, color correction, and lighting compensation. Rather than buy one screw-in glass filter of each color for each different-sized lens, most photographers use *gel* filters. These gels, actually thin sheets of dyed gelatin, are available in squares of several sizes for a fraction of the cost of glass filters.

If you use a filter infrequently, tape the filter over the front of your lens when you need it. Be careful not to get the tape in the light path. Outdoors where wind and the elements threaten the gel, tape it to the rear of the lens where it is protected inside the bellows. Gel filters are expected to succumb to use, becoming scratched and damaged with age and use. If you use filters more regularly, or need more than one at a time, you should have one of the several different kinds of filter holders available to hold them to the lens. Even though gels are less expensive than glass filters, you still will not want to replace them too often; they will last much longer if you use a filter holder instead of tape.

Some filter holders simply hold the filter in front of the lens; some include flaps to function as a lens shade. Other holders clip onto the lens and will fit lenses of several different diameters. The most secure connection is made by screwing a filter holder into the threaded front of the lens, but this requires an adapter for each lens diameter. A *compendium bellows* (p. 155) also includes a provision for holding filters.

The gel filter holder on the lens incorporates adjustable black flaps to help shade the lens and reduce flare.

If you have the time to disassemble your camera before packing it, you can store or carry it in an attaché case like this one.

Protective but bulky, a camera case like this stores the camera ready to be mounted on the tripod.

Camera Cases

Unfortunately for the user, view cameras present an awkward problem when they have to be shipped or stored. Many cameras are irregularly shaped and the ground glass is fragile. Most monorail cameras cannot be set down in a stable position on a flat surface. If your camera stays in the studio, you may just want to leave it on a tripod draped with the darkcloth when not in use. If you work on location, a field or press camera is desirable because they fold into a compact, protected box.

A monorail camera must be at least partially disassembled to assume a compact shape, and some manufacturers provide attaché-like cases to carry the pieces conveniently. If you want to take the camera out of its case ready to go on the tripod, it must be suspended upside down by its rail in a specially made box. These cases are available from camera manufacturers and accessory companies, or you may have one custom-made by a trunk or case maker. Fiberboard, aluminum, and plywood are commonly used for constructing camera cases, and you will find increased protection comes with either higher price or greater weight. Wheels on a camera case will also help you.

Film Holders

Double Sheet-Film Holder. The standard film for view cameras is sheet film, and the standard holder is a sheet-film holder. The double sheet-film holder pictured here is ubiquitous, but as you will see in the next few sections, it is by no means your only option. Film holders are designed to prevent stray light from striking the film during use or storage. They are most often made of plastic; metal holders are available at three times the price but do not function any better.

Each of the double sheet-film holder's two faces holds one sheet of film under a darkslide to protect the sheet until you are ready to expose it. Each film holder will hold no more than two sheets of film and must be unloaded and reloaded in the dark before reuse. When you are shooting in the studio, you can have ready as many holders as you care to own. In the field, excess film adds considerable unwanted weight and bulk.

The main function of this and any other film holder is to hold the film flat and in place, that is, in the same plane as the front surface of the ground glass. Plate holders, similar in appearance to film holders, are designed to hold an emulsion-coated glass plate at the film plane. Trying to use a plate holder for sheet film will result in poor focus because the thinner film will be held in the wrong position. Be careful when buying used holders not to confuse the two types.

Each face of your film holder has a flap at the bottom to fold down out of the way so you can slip in the film. At the top of each side of the holder is a slot lined with a light trap of black cloth. The darkslide is inserted through this slot and seated in the bottom flap. The bottom flap and the light-trap slot can leak light if worn, as can the darkslide if cracked or chipped. Carefully inspect these areas on any holders you buy used, and occasionally check all your holders as they age. See how to test and repair holders in Chapter 9.

On the top edge of each double film holder is a pair of small wire clips. These clips provide a safeguard against the unintentional removal of a darkslide. After you load each holder, rotate the clips into a position that blocks the movement of the darkslides. Move the clip out of the way before withdrawing a darkslide for exposure, and relock that side afterwards. You may wish to use the locks only for exposed film, since a forgotten lock may cause you to move the camera out of position inadvertently by trying to withdraw a locked darkslide before exposure.

Grafmatic Film Holders. Only slightly thicker than a double sheet-film holder, a *Grafmatic* film holder can be loaded with six sheets of film, each held in a *septum* — a thin metal separator. The Grafmatic is a boon to any itinerant photographer, since it offers a tremendous saving in space and weight over double sheet-film holders. The Graflex Sub Sea Company currently manufactures Grafmatic backs for 4x5. This company is a descendent of the original manufacturer, Graflex, Inc. Many of the original backs are still in use, and are often available secondhand. Before purchasing a used Grafmatic, check for the label *"45" Graphic*, which will ensure compatibility with any contemporary spring back. Grafmatics were also made to fit an earlier clip-in (nonspring) style back, and are marked *"45" Graflex*. These holders are unlikely to be useful unless you are using an older Graflex camera.

Practice working with an unloaded holder in the light until you understand its mechanism and idiosyncrasies. The following description may be difficult to follow unless

Other than their size, double sheet-film holders are basically identical from 2 1/4 x 3 1/4 (top) through 11x14.

The small wires at the top of each holder can be used to lock the darkslide against inadvertent withdrawal.

you have a Grafmatic in your hands as you read. Withdraw the darkslide to allow the holder's internal springs to push the stack of septa up, leaving the top septum holding a practice sheet of film in the correct position for exposure. Insert the darkslide. Notice that it slips behind the top sheet, enclosing the five others in an inner drawer covered by the darkslide. At this point, with the holder loaded and in your camera, you would ordinarily make the exposure. Withdraw the darkslide again, while you press in the small

A Grafmatic film holder holds six sheets of film, each in an individual metal septum.

If you want to use 4x5 Tri-X and travel light, find a pack film adapter to hold sixteen sheets in the space of one double holder.

clip at the side of the darkslide handle. This clip causes the drawer to slide out with the darkslide, and the top septum, left behind, will be forced to the back by springs.

Replace the darkslide and drawer, which now move as one piece. The first sheet is now at the bottom of the stack, and removing the darkslide will bring up the next sheet to be exposed. A counter, visible from the back, imprints the number (1–6) on each film sheet's edge as it is exposed. When the last of the six sheets is returned to the stack,

an X appears on the frame counter indicating a fully exposed holder. At this point the clip latches so that the darkslide will not come out without the drawer.

With the holder in the spring back ready for use, you won't be able to watch the operation of the mechanism. The darkslide may be in, appearing to cover the film, while the film is in fact in position for exposure. Without some form of indicator, this ambiguity could lead to an error. So when the top sheet in the holder is in position for exposure, either with the darkslide out or behind the top septum, a red flag appears on the back of the holder to indicate that the film is ready. When the film is covered by the darkslide, the red flag does not show, and it is safe to remove the holder from the camera.

If you change your mind and decide not to expose a film sheet after it is in position for exposure, you cannot cover that sheet again with the darkslide without sending the unexposed sheet to the bottom of the stack. To return it to the top, you must cycle the holder through all six sheets while it is on the camera. Only when the holder is in place on the camera (with the shutter closed) or in the darkroom can you cycle the septa without exposing the film.

To remove all of the film after exposure, manually advance the counter away from the X, to release the clip. Then, holding the clip in to couple the darkslide with the drawer, pull out the drawer. Push the darkslide handle in slightly to release the clip and pull out the darkslide. The six septa will rise at the end nearest the darkslide and you can remove them in a stack.

Film Packs. You may be one of that special breed ready to climb Mt. Fuji or trek through Nepal with a field camera in your backpack. For such special occasions when space and weight are *really* at a premium, or for those times when loading film is impossible, you may be pleased to discover *pack film.* Pack film is a large-format film system similar in operation to standard 35mm film: a prepackaged sequence of exposures in a lighttight cassette. The pack itself is a lighttight package of sixteen film sheets alternating with paper interleaves in a metal case designed to fit into a *film pack adapter.* This adapter in turn fits into your camera's spring back. Kodak is currently the only manufacturer of film in packs. They produce only Tri-X black-and-white film, and that only in

4x5. The pack adapter is no longer manufactured, but so few photographers use pack film that secondhand adapters in good condition are plentiful and inexpensive.

The film's standard Tri-X emulsion is coated on a very thin plastic base, so the entire package — adapter and pack with sixteen sheets of film — is no thicker than a standard double sheet-film holder. The pack is designed to be loaded into and unloaded from the holder in daylight, and after exposure the film can remain safely stored in the pack until processing. The adapter is a simple shell designed to hold the pack, fit the camera back, and provide a darkslide.

To load the adapter, remove a film pack from its foil wrapper and enclose it in the adapter with the pack's exposed paper flaps protruding through the end of the adapter away from its hinge. This may be done safely in daylight. With the adapter's darkslide in place, pull the first flap straight out and tear it off. The flap is glued at its hidden end to the first sheet of film, which is thin enough to be pulled from the back to the front of the pack around one end. Place the adapter in your camera's spring back and remove the darkslide to reveal the first sheet for exposure. Pulling the second numbered flap brings up the next sheet ready for exposure.

When all sixteen sheets are exposed and ready for processing, pull apart the thin metal pack in the dark and separate the film from the interleaving sheets. Each sheet of film is glued to an interleaving sheet along one short edge, and they should be pulled apart at that glue strip. Since the glue is water-soluble, any remaining paper adhering to the film will float off in the presoak. There will be no code notches, and you have to use your sense of touch to tell paper from film and emulsion from support. The sheets of pack film are slightly larger than standard 4x5 cut film and will not fit in standard hangers, so it is probably best to develop pack film in trays. Be extremely careful, however, because the thin base makes the sheets hard to handle and with very thin, flexible film it is difficult to keep the corners of one sheet from scratching another.

Roll Film. Although your view camera was designed to use sheet film, it may be easily adapted to use convenient roll film with a *roll film adapter*. The largest commonly available roll film is 120 size, and the adapters are made to fit 4x5 Graflok or other 4x5 spring

This roll-film adapter from Sinar fits a 4x5 spring back and can vary its format to make 4.5x6, 6x6, 6x7, 6x9, or 6x12cm negatives on 120 or 220 roll film.

backs, so using roll film means you will be reducing your large-format camera to medium-format. You will sacrifice the quality of the larger film for the convenience of roll film but will still retain the other advantages of a view camera.

There are two basic styles of roll film adapters for the use of 120 film in a 4x5 camera. One style threads the film from one end of the adapter to the other, around the other end, and back, so that both the supply and takeup spools of the film are at one end of the adapter. This kind of adapter can be made thin enough to fit in the spring back like a sheet-film holder. The other style, with the spools at opposite ends of the holder, replaces the spring back in a Graflok (or universal) back. The former is harder to load, but may be used without removing the ground glass each time after focusing. These adapters are made to accommodate 120 and 220 film, which are the same width but different lengths, and to make negatives in 6x7, 6x9, and 6x12cm formats.

If you wish to use roll film in a camera larger than 4x5, your camera may have a *reducing back* available as an option. A reducing back is made to fit the back of some 5x7 or 8x10 cameras and provide a 4x5 spring back in the center of the larger frame. These backs are necessary if you wish to use 4x5 Polaroid products (see the following section) in a larger camera.

Minor White took this photograph in 1973 on Type 52 Polaroid film. The finished print can be viewed in 20 seconds, allowing the results of one photograph to contribute to the next.

A very few highly specialized aerial cameras use roll film in widths of 70mm (the same as 120), 5 inch, and $9\frac{1}{2}$ inch. A discussion of their use is beyond the scope of this book.

Polaroid Films

Photography really came out of the dark ages in 1947, the year Dr. Edwin Land used an 8x10 view camera to demonstrate the first Polaroid self-developing film. It is difficult to comprehend, let alone summarize, the effect instant photography has had on the medium. Within ten years, Polaroid had firmly established an amateur market, selling well over a million cameras. By now nearly everyone, worldwide, has had some experience with Polaroid's amateur products as the photographer, subject, or observer of a pictorial near-miracle. Using instant film, people no longer need to wonder whether the picture will "come out."

Much less well known, yet responsible for dramatic changes in the lives of professional photographers everywhere, are Polaroid's large-format products. Before Land's introduction of a 4x5 holder and sheet film in 1958, a photographer's test exposure was always followed by a lengthy interruption for processing. In the studio, this limitation dampened enthusiasm for exploring lighting options, especially in the presence of a client. On location or in the field, the photographer always felt the need to ensure results with redundant exposures made with several different apertures and several different filters. Now a black-and-white print in 15 seconds (color in 60 seconds) gives us all the infor-

In Laura's Feet, 1973, *Rosamond Wolff Purcell takes advantage of the ability of Type 52 film to render delicate light tones.*

mation we need about lighting, exposure, focus, and composition — indeed, it may give us the final product itself.

4x5 Sheet Film

The first system of products Polaroid developed specifically for professional and technical use was the sheet film and holder for 4x5 cameras. Still in production, this film system uses single-exposure lighttight packets, each containing a positive sheet, negative sheet, and development chemical (Polaroid calls it a *reagent*) pod. These packets are sold in boxes of twenty, and may be removed from the box, loaded, and developed in the light.

The original #500 film holder was supplanted by the #545 in 1968. Both were designed to be inserted into the spring back of any standard 4x5 camera. Each holder contains a pair of stainless steel rollers to break the chemical pod and spread the processing *goo* (an unofficial Polaroid term) evenly between positive and negative for development. The rollers are engaged by a lever on the outside of the holder.

The Polaroid #545 film holder adapts their single-sheet films to a 4x5 spring back.

To load a sheet of 4x5 Polaroid film, set the lever on the film holder to L, for Load. Notice that one end of the film sheet has a metal clip. Insert this end of the film into the open end of the holder and slide the film down until the clip clicks into place and will go no farther. One side of the film packet, imprinted with the phrase "This side toward lens," should be visible through the open face of the holder when the film is properly loaded. Handle the film only by its edges and be particularly careful with the area of the packet surrounding the chemical pod. This area is slightly thicker than the rest of the sheet and is printed with a warning label.

When your camera is set for an exposure, insert the Polaroid holder as you would a standard holder into the spring back of your camera, making sure the open side of the holder faces the lens. The #545 holder can also clip into the place of the spring back in a universal (or Graflok) back. After checking to make sure the shutter is closed and the holder is properly seated, pull the exposed end of the film packet straight out until it stops. You have withdrawn the lighttight envelope that contains the positive sheet, and

Place the holder on a steady, flat surface and hold it in place firmly as you pull the packet through the rollers for processing. Leaving the holder in the camera for this operation risks jarring the camera out of position.

left the clip, negative, and chemical pod inside the holder. This is equivalent to withdrawing the darkslide from a sheet-film holder.

Make the exposure, then push the film envelope back into its original position and remove the holder from the camera. Swing the lever on the holder to P, for Process, and lay the holder on the edge of a flat surface as shown. Setting the lever to P engages the roller assembly at the top of the holder, pressing the rollers together. Secure the holder with one hand, grasp the end of the film packet with the other, and pull the packet straight out of the holder through the rollers. The pulling motion should be very steady and neither too slow nor too fast; it should take about 1/2 second to slide the packet all the way through the rollers. Pulling the packet through the rollers breaks the pod of chemical reagent and spreads it between negative and positive as they are pressed together. As the negative develops, a process called *diffusion* transfers the image across the developer layer to the positive.

Begin timing the development just as the film leaves the rollers. Each type of film has its appropriate development time printed on each packet. A few seconds before the processing time elapses, peel apart the packet to reveal the negative/positive sandwich inside. Peel up a corner of the white positive sheet and separate it from the rest of the sandwich with a snap of your wrist at the moment the development time should end. Take care not to get any of the caustic developing reagent on your hands or clothing, and wash it off immediately if you do.

Type 52. The first Polaroid 4x5 film was Type 52 and it is still the most popular of their professional products. Introduced in 1958 along with the #500 holder, the early T-52 produced a black-and-white print in 60 seconds. Its film speed was increased from 200 to 400 in 1961, and the development time was reduced to 15 seconds. The resulting print is very fine-grained, with a beautiful tonal scale, and the film is capable of very high resolution. For permanence, however, the print must be coated after development using the coating fluid and applicator supplied with the film.

Type 52 film is ideal for proofing in the studio. Not only is it useful for judging exposure and checking composition before a final shot, but it is indispensable as a means to test

Philippe Halsman made these two photographs on Type 52 as a test when shooting Jantzen Swimsuits for Life *magazine in 1959.*

each step in setting up complicated lighting or multiple exposures. You may wish to use T-52 as a proofing system for another film with a different speed, for example, a color negative or transparency film. If you do, use a neutral-density (ND) filter to compensate for the different light sensitivity rather than changing light or camera settings. You will then be able to see the exact depth of field and lighting ratios in the test that you will see in the final shot.

Use the following chart to select an appropriate neutral-density filter for alternate final films. These will match a T-52 proof to a slower final product (no practical large-format films are faster). Place the filter over your lens when exposing the Type 52 and be sure to remove it before switching films.

Film Speed	ND
320	.1
125	.5
100	.6
64	.8
50	.9

A neutral-density filter will reduce the intensity of light without affecting its color. A ND .3 filter will withhold one stop of light, that is, it will reduce the light by half. A .6 neutral density will be the same as two .3 filters superimposed; the first will reduce the light by half and the second will reduce what's left by half. So a .6 filter will transmit 25 percent of the light; it will reduce it by two stops. Each .1 increment in density is equal to 1/3 stop.

When you use Polaroid's products for a proofing system, remember that the shape and dimensions of the Polaroid print will not match exactly those of conventional film. A simple test procedure, photographing a flat page from a newspaper on both types of film, will allow you to mark the ground glass of your camera with the exact edges of each format.

Type 57. Introduced in 1961, Type 57 is a very high speed black-and-white film for general purpose photography. Although it does not have the pictorial elegance of Type 52, at 3000 ASA it is useful for a number of scientific and technical applications.

Type 55. In the earliest days of their 4x5 products, Polaroid made Type 52 for a black-and-white print, and Type 53, which produced a black-and-white negative. In 1961 they introduced Type 55, which produces a finished print and fully developed negative simultaneously in 20 seconds. The published film speed is 50, but using 32 will yield a better negative (and a worse print). The print must be coated for permanence, and the negative must be cleared of the chemical reagent within a few minutes after development by immersion in a saturated solution of sodium sulfite for one minute. For work in the field, however, the negative may remain safely immersed in the sulfite clearing solution for several days. Once removed from the clearing solution, the negative needs only to be washed and dried like any conventional black-and-white negative.

Types 58 and 59. Introduced in 1962 as *Polacolor*, Type 58 4x5 film makes a color print in 60 seconds. It requires no treatment after development, but a color shift occurs upon drying, so delay judgment of color balance a minute or two after peeling the print.

Type 59, or *Polacolor 2*, has been available since 1975, and is a lower-contrast version of Polacolor. Both versions are tailored to studio conditions and perform optimally when exposed with electronic flash and processed at room temperature.

Professional Chrome. The newest of Polaroid's 4x5 products, introduced in 1986, *Professional Chrome* is their first non-self-developing film. It is a conventional E-6 Process color reversal (transparency) film, packaged in individual opaque envelopes that fit their #545 holder. Loading the film into the holder, as with the instant 4x5 films, is a daylight operation, and you need only the one holder, no matter how much film you use.

Pack Films

The roll film used in Polaroid's first amateur cameras required the negative and positive to remain in contact for development inside the camera. With the introduction of the pack film format in 1963, it was no longer necessary to wait for complete processing before making another exposure. Once a sheet of this pack film is exposed, the negative/posi-

Mark Klett's 1983 photo-graph Picnic on the edge of the rim, Grand Canyon, **AZ** *is an en-largement made from a Type 55 instant negative. He used a lens tilt to move the plane of focus into a horizontal position, stretching from his feet in the foreground to the op-posite rim of the canyon.*

tive sandwich can be pulled out of the camera through rollers, beginning the processing outside the camera. The packs, containing eight positive and eight negative sheets, were originally made to fit only Polaroid cameras containing built-in roller assemblies.

Polaroid introduced the Model #405 film pack adapter in 1974 to extend the usefulness of what by then was a full line of pack films. This adapter enabled photographers to use the series 100 (now series 600) pack films in conventional 4x5 cameras. The finished prints from pack films are smaller than 4x5 (about 72x95mm, or $2\frac{7}{8}$x$3\frac{3}{4}$ inches), so with the purchase of each film holder Polaroid includes an acetate template made to fit a 4x5 ground glass with position marks for the pack film format. The #405 holder incorporates a darkslide to allow removal of the holder from the camera for focusing and adjustment between exposures.

Because the film packs were adapted to and not designed for the view camera, the holder is too thick to fit easily into all spring backs. And when it does fit, its thickness demands that you take special care when inserting the holder to avoid jarring the camera. The holder was designed with side slots to allow it to clip into a universal back in place of the spring back.

Polaroid films available in packs correspond to their 4x5 films: Type 662 is 400 speed black-and-white print film identical to Type 52 (although it requires no coating after development), Type 665 is positive/negative, and Types 668 and 669 are Polacolor 1 and 2.

4x5 Pack Film. In 1981, Polaroid introduced a larger version of pack film specifically for the professional market. These convenient pack films in full 4x5 size require the Model 550 film holder to adapt them to a conventional 4x5 spring (or universal) back. Films available for use in the Model 550 include Type 552 (the pack version of Type 52) and Type 559 (Polacolor 2). Like the Model 405 holder, the 550 loads rapidly with prepackaged packs, has a built-in roller system that is removable for cleaning, and incorporates a darkslide. The product illustrations for this book were made on Type 552 (and 52) film and are reproduced directly from the 4x5 Polaroid prints. This process saved the author countless hours of darkroom work.

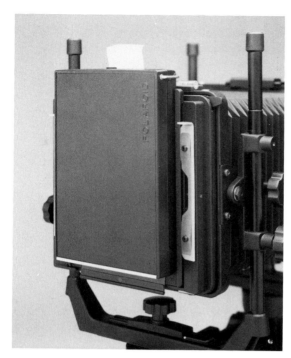

This Polaroid #405 Pack Film Adapter is held to the camera by the clips on the universal (Graflok) back.

Polaroid's #550 Pack Film Adapter holds packs that each make eight instant 4x5 prints.

The 8x10 System

Professional photographers who need a finished product without delay can use Polaroid's 8x10 system. Like the other professional products from Polaroid, the 8x10 system includes both positive and negative sheets, development chemicals in a pod, a roller assembly to burst the pod for processing, and an adapter to fit the system to a conventional view camera. The resulting 8x10 prints can go home with the client, be placed on display immediately, or be used as the original for high-quality offset lithography. An 8x10 print is large enough to be a satisfactory final product for many of the needs of portrait or commercial photographers, and an instant 8x10 print is also useful for making proofs for critical 8x10 work with conventional films.

Although the positive and negative sheets are packaged separately, each film available for Polaroid's 8x10 system is basically a larger version of one of their 4x5 products. The 8x10 system's film holder (Model 81-06) accepts one sheet of negative material at a time for exposure in a conventional 8x10 camera. After exposure, you slip the positive sheet with its attached chemical pod into the holder, and insert the package into the electrically powered 81-12 Processor. Rollers large enough to distribute the developing reagent evenly across the 8-inch width are too heavy to be incorporated into the holder, and the separate, motor-driven processor ensures that the film will pass through the rollers at a constant and correct speed. Its built-in timer starts automatically and informs you when the selected processing time has elapsed.

Optional Camera Parts

Bellows

The bellows on your camera is not an accessory, but a necessary part of the camera. Your camera probably was supplied with an accordion-fold standard bellows as original equipment. The standard bellows for 4x5 cameras is square in cross section (it is also called a *square* bellows), and is the same size at the front and rear. Larger cameras most often have tapered standard bellows, still square in cross section but smaller at the front. A tapered bellows will collapse into a shorter package than a square bellows.

The 8x10 system from Polaroid uses a separate motor-driven processor to ensure correct roller pressure and even development. The film holder shown here with the processor adapts the Polaroid negative to a standard 8x10 spring back.

Bag Bellows. If your camera's bellows is removable and sold as part of a modular camera system, you will have the option of buying and using a *bag* or *wide-angle* bellows. Bag bellows is an appropriate name for the amorphous mass of black material that replaces the traditional accordion folds of a square bellows. It is needed when you use short focal-length lenses because the short back-focus distance (image distance) of a wide-angle lens requires that the front and rear standards be quite close together — close enough that most accordion bellows would be compressed almost totally. A square bellows closed all the way becomes quite rigid, and prevents use of the camera movements. In fact, very short focal-length lenses often cannot be brought close enough to the film plane to focus at infinity with the square bellows in place. The bag bellows, however, offers no restrictions on movements and will allow the front and rear standards to be as close together as the design of the camera permits. Use of the bag bellows is limited to short focal-length lenses because of its short maximum extension.

Extra Bellows. Very long lenses, or extreme close-ups, can require another bellows option available only for a modular monorail camera. When one bellows will not extend enough for a particular use, a second may be added by sliding another standard onto the

Not available in camera stores yet no longer a research lab curiosity, this huge view camera was built by Polaroid's technicians to make instant 20x24-inch color prints. This photograph of the author using the camera was made by John Reuter, the manager of the New York studio in which the camera is based.

This photograph of the Fuller Building, with the General Motors Building in the background, was made by Reinhart Wolf for his 1980 book New York *(original in color).*

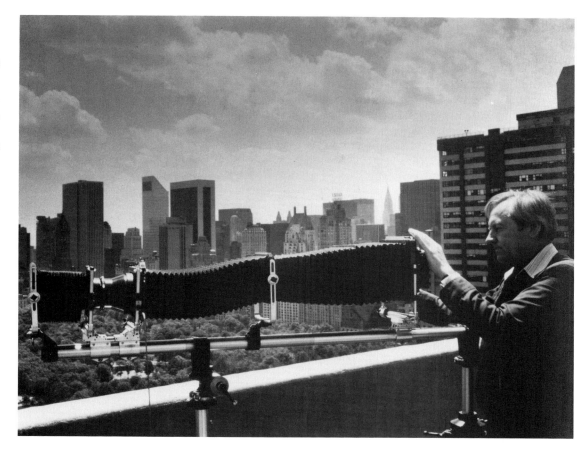

German photographer Reinhart Wolf is shown photographing the top of a skyscraper. His 1000mm lens required an extra standard and bellows on his 8x10 Sinar. The third bellows at the extreme left is a compendium lens shade. This photograph is by Geoff Juckes.

Using a wide-angle lens is much more convenient with a bag bellows and short monorail like on this Toyo.

rail into a position between the front and rear standards. Since the clips on both sides of the standards are the same, this center standard may be used to connect the rear of one bellows to the front of another.

Compendium Bellows. Another optional bellows, called a *compendium* bellows, fits over the lens to be used as a shade and works to accommodate the camera movements in a way that a fixed lens shade cannot. While you view through the ground glass, you may adjust the compendium's extension to the correct length for a lens of any focal length and match any camera movements with the compendium's own front swing and tilt. Keeping stray light from falling on the front of the lens during exposure will reduce image-degrading flare; the compendium should shade the lens by being extended as far as possible without vignetting (blocking part of the image). Vignetting can be seen in the corners and edges of the ground glass as shaded parts in the image itself. Once adjusted, the compendium can be moved on its hinges up out of the way of the lens so you can adjust the aperture and set and wind the shutter. The black accordion folds of its inner surface, like the interior of the camera's bellows, act as a baffle to reduce unwanted light reflection. Many models of compendium bellows include a convenient drawer across the front of the bellows for holding a filter, but they require a larger, more expensive gel than those you can attach to the front of the lens.

Ground Glass

The ground glass supplied with your camera is relatively easy to replace. And since it is the most fragile part of your camera, it may not be long before you need to find out just *how* easy. You may also want to replace the screen with one of the optional styles to better suit your needs.

The most simple ground glass is a plain, unmarked rectangle cut in the correct dimensions to fit into the spring back's frame on your camera's back. Many plain ground-glass screens have cut corners that serve two purposes. First, if your camera does not incorporate lighttrap air vents in the standards, these cuts are necessary to allow air to flow in and out of the camera's interior when the bellows is moved during setup or focusing. Second, you may look through these triangular openings to see the rear of the lens.

By looking at the shape of the diaphragm visible from a corner of the back, you will be able to identify vignetting by the lens barrel, filter, lens shade, or a bend in the bellows. Vignetting is often the result of using camera movements too extreme for the coverage of the lens; some of the ground glass will be outside the image circle. When there is no interference, the open diaphragm set at the working aperture should appear oval and symmetrical when viewed from a corner. Vignetting will cause this oval to be shaded, to be asymmetrical, or to have pointed ends. In an extreme case, the diaphragm may not be visible at all. If your ground glass does not have cut corners, you can do the job yourself if you are handy with a glass cutter. Unfortunately, cut corners also remove part of the image from view.

A less common ground-glass style has a clear, unground spot or circle with fine cross hairs in its center for *aerial image* focusing. You focus while looking at the cross hairs, and the lens image is projected through the glass and focused directly by your eye. When the cross hairs and aerial image (the one

The compendium bellows is a lens shade that is adjustable to accommodate camera movements.

A magnifying loupe makes precise focusing easier.

Loupes intended for viewing slides are satisfactory for view camera focusing. The compact loupe on the left was designed for view camera use and can be worn around your neck on a string.

This replacement 4x5 ground glass has an etched grid, cut corners, and framing marks for roll film.

from the camera's lens) are in focus simultaneously, the image distance (or focus) is correct. A low-power magnifier, or *loupe*, will aid in focusing with either screen. Some photographers, particularly in technical or scientific work, find aerial image focusing to be more precise than plain ground-glass focusing.

All lenses project less light to the edges than to the center, and light at the edges of the frame is angled away from your eyes. An accessory *fresnel* lens, or screen, attached to the rear of your ground glass, or an optional ground glass incorporating such a screen, will more evenly illuminate the entire image area. The screen is actually a simple plano-convex lens sectioned into flat, concentric rings, and it directs the light leaving the ground glass into parallel rays. Without a fresnel (pronounced frĕ-nĕl') screen, you may have difficulty seeing the corners of your ground-glass image.

Another useful addition to the standard ground glass is a grid of horizontal and vertical lines etched or printed on its surface to aid in precise image alignment. A transparent plastic overlay with the same rulings can be taped in place to serve the same purpose, and can be removed when not needed. Other ruled lines are also useful to mark the borders of another film size or format, such as Polaroid 4x5 film, which produces an image that is slightly smaller than 4x5 and is not centered in the frame.

You may be able to find an accessory ground glass with the appropriate markings, or you may have to add them to yours with a permanent marker. Temporary marks may be made directly on the ground glass with a china-marking crayon. Advertising photography often requires making a photograph to match an art-director's layout exactly. To make this job easier, a china-marking crayon or washable felt-tip pen can be used to sketch the layout with removable marks on a plastic overlay, or upside down directly on the ground glass.

Lensboards

Since it is much easier to replace the board in the camera than the lens in the board, you will need one *lensboard* for each lens you use frequently. Most lensboards are square and symmetrical and clip easily into the front standard of the camera for which they were made. Each board should have a center hole of the correct diameter drilled or punched for

The final use of Grohe's photograph, a magazine cover, shows how areas in the photograph were deliberately held open for type. The empty space at the lower left is for the mailing label.

This complicated montage was planned out methodically in advance. The art director sketched the placement of objects on the ground glass and photographer Steve Grohe made the final image with multiple exposures on a single sheet of film.

The smaller, silver-colored lensboard is a Graphic board, which also fits an early Toyo Field. Here it is clipped in place in an adapter lensboard on a Toyo View.

A recessed lensboard can overcome some of a camera's physical obstructions to the use of short-focal-length lenses.

the shutter to be mounted in it. There are three standard shutter sizes:

#0 35mm   #1 42mm   #3 65.5mm

Many shutters use the head of a small screw as an alignment pin. The screw fits into a small hole in the lensboard just outside the edge of the center hole. This arrangement prevents the shutter from rotating in its mount.

Lensboards are made in a variety of mutually incompatible sizes and contours. Unlike the film back, no universal design for lensboards has ever been accepted. Only occasionally are the boards of one manufacturer interchangeable with another — for example Sinar with Horseman, Linhof with Wista and Tachihara, and Graphic with Toyo. Many manufacturers make adapter boards which can be invaluable to anyone owning more than one camera. Usually they adapt a smaller board, such as a 4-inch-square Calumet to a larger opening for an 8-inch-square Toyo board. If you interchange lenses among several cameras, it is often wise to mount all your lenses on identical small boards, such as Toyo/Graphic or Calumet, and use an adapter to mount the small boards onto each camera.

Many times the design of a camera or the bulk of a bellows prevent the front and rear standards from being placed closely enough to focus a wide-angle lens. Special *recessed* lensboards accommodate very short focal-length lenses. A recessed lensboard holds the lens behind the normal position, preventing the bellows from compressing into inflexibility. Access to the shutter settings and cable-release mount can be restricted by a recessed board, sometimes necessitating special linkages and extensions.

David Graham used a front tilt on his 8x10 camera to make the plane of focus cut through the toys and hose and the figure in the background (original in color).

9 Maintenance

Once you have acquired the equipment for large-format photography, you will want to keep all of the pieces in good working order. Well-made cameras, lenses, and accessories have a long working life, but careless operation and the lack of routine maintenance can degrade the quality of your work and shorten the useful life of your expensive equipment. Occasional but regular attention should be sufficient, but the cardinal rule is this: keep it clean. Dust and dirt will paralyze shutters and focusing gears, create annoying marks on film, and impair the sharpness of a lens. A few simple precautions will protect your investment in equipment and ensure quality in your results.

Lenses

The front and rear surfaces of your lens are exposed and fragile. Keep them covered with lens caps whenever the lens is not in use and dust the lens only when necessary. Try a gentle blast from a compressed gas sprayer or an air syringe to remove loose dust. Be very careful with sprayers containing hydrocar-

When using compressed gas spray dusters to clean your camera equipment, be very careful to hold the can vertically to avoid spraying the gas in liquid form.

bons, such as Dust-Off. If you don't hold the can vertically, the gas can come out as a very cold liquid, leaving a permanent frost mark on your lens. Never blow on a lens. Your breath is never free of tiny bits of saliva that will leave spots on your lens.

If compressed air doesn't remove the dust, you can use a brush on your lens. Use only a very clean, very soft camel's hair brush and brush gently. To avoid transferring oil to the lens, don't touch the bristles with your fingers. Never use a cloth or tissue to remove dust. Dust particles trapped under a cloth create a fine sandpaper, and you will abrade the lens' delicate surface. Modern lenses have a fragile antireflection coating that can be damaged more easily than the glass itself.

Never use silicone-treated eyeglass or record cleaning cloths on your photographic lenses. They will smear and degrade the coating. If a fingerprint or greasy smear appears on your lens, clean it with an untreated lint-free tissue (such as Kodak lens-cleaning tissue) and a few drops of a good lens cleaning liquid (also Kodak) or pharmaceutical methyl alcohol. Since liquids dripped on the lens can seep past the edge seal into the lens barrel, apply the liquid to the tissue, not directly onto the lens. Dust your lens with compressed air before attempting to remove a fingerprint, and don't allow any fingerprints to remain on the lens for long. The natural acidity of your skin trapped in a greasy print will etch the lens coating, making the mark permanent.

Handle your lenses carefully to avoid dropping them. When installing a lens, make sure the lensboard is properly seated and clipped into place. Vibration or jarring can loosen lens elements in the barrel or separate cemented groups. If an element moves slightly out of its correct position, the lens has *decentered* and its optical performance will suffer. A professional repair service can test a lens for proper centering. Whenever your lenses are not in use, they should be stored in a plastic bag to keep out dust. For further protection, wrap the plastic bag containing the lens in its plastic bag with soft cloth, leather, foam, or bubble-wrap.

If you wish to mount or remove a lens from its board, use a *spanner wrench*. This wrench is a special tool used to remove the retaining ring that holds the shutter or barrel to the lensboard. Its two blades fit into opposing slots on the perimeter of the retaining ring, allowing you to unscrew the ring without unnecessary hazard to the lens. It is easy to damage an expensive lens trying to remove a retaining ring with an improper tool. The spanner wrench can be adjusted to fit retaining rings on any common lens. Along with the spanner in your studio toolbox should be a set of small jeweler's screwdrivers. These are handy to keep all the tiny screws on your shutter-mounted lenses properly tightened.

The back of the lensboard and lens, the side facing the film, should be nonreflective. The original black surface will eventually wear or chip, leading to image flare. Keep a small bottle of flat black paint on hand for touch-ups. Kodak Brushing Lacquer No. 4, Dull Black, is a product made specifically for this application.

Store your lenses in plastic bags when not in use.

Shutters

Dust is your shutter's worst enemy. Always store all your shutter-mounted lenses in plastic bags. Disuse can cause your shutter to slow and stick, but a few cycles of winding and releasing can sometimes remedy these problems. Never store your shutters in the wound position. The tension on the spring will eventually cause it to stretch and slow the speeds.

Some shutters, notably Compurs, use an extra spring to provide sufficient tension for their highest speed. Your shutter has this extra spring if the highest speed setting on the dial is spaced farther apart from the others, and if turning the dial to this setting requires more force to set the additional spring. These shutters can be severely damaged by changing the speed setting when the shutter is tensioned. To avoid damage with this shutter, always release it before changing speeds.

Shutters have two particularly vulnerable points. The cable-release attachment point is easy to damage on most shutters, particularly by pulling on the cable release. Either remove the cable release or make sure there is

Use a spanner wrench to remove and replace the retaining ring that holds a lens to its board.

Never pull on an attached cable release. The attachment point is the most vulnerable part of a shutter.

no pressure on the attachment point when wrapping the lens for storage. A shutter's other weak spot is the threaded lens mount. Pushing on or jarring a lens, particularly a wasp-waisted wide-field, can bend or twist the mount and leave the lens out of alignment. Always handle your lenses gently and store them carefully.

Never attempt to repair, dismantle, or lubricate a shutter yourself. Always take it to a trained professional in a repair shop. It is embarrassing to bring in a bag containing most of the shutter's parts after you have removed the faceplate and watched the springs fly across the room. A professional repair shop will usually test the shutter speeds for accuracy for a nominal fee. A shutter's inaccuracies are usually consistent, and if you know those for your shutter you can compensate for them in exposure.

Film Holders

Light can leak into holders from worn felt light traps and cracked darkslides. If you suspect that one of your holders leaks, or if you buy used holders, test them before you entrust them with an important exposure. To test a film holder for leaks, cut a sheet of black-and-white printing paper to size, insert it in the holder, and leave the closed holder in a brightly lit place for an hour or two, turning the holder occasionally to expose all sides to light. Unless you test only one side of one holder at a time, mark the back of the sheet with a permanent marker or cut a corner to identify the holder and side. You can use film for your testing, but paper is less expensive and can be handled in safelight. Any holders to be used with infrared film should be tested for leaks with that film before using; infrared radiation can penetrate some darkslides that are opaque to the visible spectrum.

After developing the test paper or film, inspect it for dark areas that indicate unwanted exposure. The presence of streaks or fog indicates light leaks and their position will reveal the location of a crack, chip, or pinhole. If you find that a holder leaks light, repair or discard it. Black photo tape can be used to patch the bottom flap, and new darkslides are available from the manufacturers of film holders. Replacement darkslides in uncommon sizes, such as those for banquet

Keep a spare brush attachment for your vacuum cleaner for cleaning only your photography gear.

The roller assemblies in Polaroid film holders need frequent cleaning. Fortunately, they are made easily accessible.

cameras, can be fabricated from sheets of black phenolic plastic available from a commercial plastic supplier.

Dust in the holders can settle on the film during exposure and produce tiny *pinholes* or clear specks on negatives and black marks on prints and transparencies. Store and transport your film holders in plastic bags, and dust each holder before loading. For thorough cleaning, buy a new brush attachment for your vacuum cleaner and use it only on camera equipment.

Polaroid holders need to be maintained regularly as well. Dust or vacuum them as you would any other holder. Before each use, inspect the rollers for bits of developing reagent that occasionally leak out of the film packs. Open the holder and clean the rollers with a damp lintless cloth or tissue. You can easily remove the roller assembly from a #405 or #550 pack adapter for cleaning, and although it is not convenient to remove the rollers from a #545 sheet-film holder, you can easily release a pair of clips to disengage them from each other for cleaning. Always store a #545 holder with its processing lever in the L position (that is, with its rollers disengaged).

Bellows

Dust from the inside of your bellows can settle on film during exposure. Stretch out the bellows periodically and vacuum the inside. Leather bellows should be treated on their outer surface with a leather preservative to prevent cracking. Light leaks in a bellows can be difficult to diagnose, producing degrading flare in some photographs but not in others. To check the bellows, set up your camera in a darkroom and extend the bellows. Remove the back and hold a flashlight inside the bellows, covering your arm and the back with a darkcloth. Pinhole leaks will be visible as you move the flashlight, and you can patch them with a dab of black silicone caulk or a small piece of black electrical tape.

Tripods

For tripods, too, dust is the enemy. If possible, remove dust from the leg segments of your tripod each time you put it away. After a year or two of use, the tripod head may not move as smoothly as it should. Using simple tools, you can dismantle the head, clean it, lubricate its sliding parts with a little auto grease, and reassemble it. The leg section clamps are usually designed to operate without additional lubricant, but you can rejuvenate them occasionally with a thorough cleaning. Naphtha or small amounts of a nonabrasive household cleanser will remove grease and oil. To avoid corrosion, never wash your tripod or immerse it in water.

Photo Credits

Unless otherwise credited, all photographs by the author.

Pages vi, 93, 95, 97, 98, 99, 101, 109, 122, 124: Equipment courtesy of the Jack Naylor Collection

Page viii: New Orleans Museum of Art, New Orleans, Louisiana

Pages 1, 18, 74, 144: Sinar Bron, Inc.

Page 4: Magnum Photos

Pages 6–11, 16, 17, 19–25, 32–33, 36–37, 50–51, 56–57, 79, 100, 106, 140–141, 156–157: Equipment courtesy of Calumet, Inc.

Page 38: U. S. Geological Survey, Denver, Colorado and Rephotographic Survey Project

Page 39: Rephotographic Survey Project

Page 70: Equipment courtesy of Ed Kostiner

Page 76: Fogg Art Museum, Harvard University

Page 96: The Denver Public Library, Western History Department

Page 97: Smithsonian Institution, Washington, D.C.

Page 100: Cameras courtesy of William Crawford and Neal Rantoul

Page 103: The Humanities Research Center, University of Texas at Austin

Page 104: The Weegee Collection

Page 105: New York *Daily News*

Pages 106, 111, 139: Equipment courtesy of E. Philip Levine

Page 107: Linhof GMBH

Page 108: Courtesy of nuArc Company, Inc. and Polaroid Corp.

Page 109: The Paul Strand Foundation

Page 110: Copyright: The Oakland Museum, The City of Oakland, 1982

Page 111: Courtesy of Peter Gowland

Pages 134–137: Equipment courtesy of Karl Heitz, Inc.

Page 138: Bela Kalman, Studio 350

Pages 145–146: Courtesy of The Polaroid Collection

Page 147: © Philippe Halsman from The Polaroid Collection

Page 152: Equipment courtesy of Stanley Rowin, Stanley Studio

Page 158: Courtesy of Digital Equipment Corp.

Courtesy of the Beverly and Jack Wilgus Collection.

Index